The GATT Negotiations 1986-90: Origins, Issues & Prospects

by Sidney Golt

BRITISH-NORTH AMERICAN COMMITTEE

Sponsored by
British-North American Research Association (UK)
National Planning Association (USA)
C. D. Howe Institute (Canada)

© British-North American Committee
Short quotations with appropriate credit permissible

ISBN 0-902594-48-6

Published by the British-North American Committee

Printed and bound in the United Kingdom by
Contemprint Limited, London SE1

November 1988

Contents

The GATT Negotiations 1986-1990:
Origins, Issues and Progress
by Sidney Golt

Appendices

Statement of the British-North American Committee to Accompany the Report

We are pleased to publish this fourth Paper in a series of publications on multilateral trade by the experienced British commentator Sidney Golt.

The first two papers[1] reported on the progress in implementing the Tokyo Round of GATT negotiations in the mid 1970s. At the start of the 1980s, Mr Golt reviewed the major outstanding trade issues that needed addressing by world statesmen[2].

The current paper has been written as a guide to the issues facing negotiators in the Uruguay Round of trade negotiations underway in Geneva. Given the background of instability in world financial markets, it is all the more important that public evidence of tangible progress should emerge from these negotiations. The Committee, after discussing the paper at a recent bi-annual meeting, is pleased to make it available to a wider audience.

----

[1] The GATT Negotiations 1973-75: A Guide to the Issues, April 1974.
   The GATT Negotiations, 1973-79: The Closing Stage, May 1979.
[2] Trade Issues in the Mid 1980s, October 1982.

Footnote to the Statement
Over the last eighteen months financial markets have been more than usually volatile. What is encouraging is that in spite of this, the growth in world trade has continued to the obvious benefit of the world economy. We consider this to be due in no small part to the effectiveness of the GATT as a framework of rules for international trade. All the more important then, that in the current round of negotiations these are extended to cover more products and services and adapted in a way which enhances trade rather than hinders it.

Sir James Ball, Roger Bexon, William McDonough, Sir Patrick Meaney,
A. B. Marshall, and William Turner.

Members of the Committee Signing the Statement

THE EARL OF AIRLIE
Chairman, General Accident Fire and Life
Assurance Corporation plc, Perth, Scotland

WILLIAM F. ANDREWS
Chairman and Chief Executive Officer,
SSMC, Inc., Shelton, CT

MICHAEL ANGUS
Chairman, Unilever plc, London

DR. DAVID ATTERTON
Director, Marks & Spencer plc, London

EDGAR L. BALL
International Secretary,
United Steelworkers of America,
AFL-CIO, CLC, Pittsburgh, PA

* PROFESSOR SIR JAMES BALL
Chairman,
Legal & General Group plc, London

NICHOLAS BARING
Deputy Chairman, Barings plc, London

FRANK BARLOW
Chief Executive,
Financial Times Ltd., London

MICHEL BELANGER
Chairman of the Board and Chief Executive
Officer,
National Bank of Canada, Montreal,
Quebec

SIR CHRISTOPHER BENSON
Chairman and Chief Executive Officer,
MEPC, London

SIR JEFFREY BENSON
Chairman,
600 Group, Herts, UK

ROGER BEXON
Chairman,
Laporte Industries (Holdings) plc,
London

CARROL D. BOLEN
Vice President,
Pioneer Hi-Bred International, Inc.,
Des Moines, IA

GEORGE J. CLARK
Executive Vice President,
Citibank, N.A.,
New York, NY

DONALD M. COX
New York, NY

PROFESSOR
SIR FREDERICK CRAWFORD
Vice Chancellor,
The University of Aston in Birmingham,
Birmingham

SIR JOHN CUCKNEY
Chairman, 3i Group plc,
London

JAMES E. CUNNINGHAM
Chairman and Chief Executive Officer,
McDermott International Inc.,
New Orleans, LA

J. V. RAYMOND CYR
President, Bell Canada Enterprise,
Montreal, Quebec

GERALD L. DENNIS
Deputy Chairman,
BAT Industries plc, London

SIR KENNETH DURHAM
Chairman, Woolworth Holdings plc,
London

GERRY EASTWOOD
Assistant General Secretary,
MSF, London

JOHN F. FRASER
President and Chief Executive Officer,
Federal Industries Ltd.,
Winnipeg, Manitoba

JOHN H. HALE
Director, Pearson plc, London

R. C. HAMPEL
Executive Director,
ICI plc, London

FRED L. HARTLEY
Chairman and Chief Executive Officer,
Unocal Corporation,
Los Angeles, CA

ARDEN R. HAYNES
Chairman, President and Chief Executive
Officer, Imperial Oil Limited,
Ontario

*See footnote to statement

DONALD J. PHILLIPS
Chairman, President and Chief Executive
Officer, Inco Limited,
Toronto, Ontario

BRIAN PITMAN
Chief Executive,
Lloyds Bank plc, London

SIR DAVID PLASTOW
Chairman and Chief Executive,
Vickers plc, London

ALFRED POWIS
Chairman and Chief Executive Officer,
Noranda Inc., Toronto, Ontario

BEN ROBERTS
Professor Emeritus,
Department of Industrial Relations,
London School of Economics, London

PROFESSOR HAROLD B. ROSE
London Business School, London

NATHANIEL SAMUELS
Managing Director,
Shearson Lehman Brothers Inc.,
New York, NY

THOMAS R. SAYLOR
Chief Executive,
Cell Systems Ltd,
Cambridge, UK

DAVID SIMON
Managing Director,
British Petroleum Company plc,
London

PROFESSOR THOMAS H. B. SYMONS
Vanier Professor,
Trent University, and Director,
Celanese Canada Inc.,
Peterborough, Ontario

ALLAN R. TAYLOR
Chairman and Chief Executive Officer,
The Royal Bank of Canada,
Toronto, Canada

KENNETH TAYLOR
Senior Vice President,
RJR Nabisco Inc,
New York, NY

E. K. TURNER
Executive Director,
Prairie Pools Inc.,
Regina, Saskatchewan

* WILLIAM I. M. TURNER, JR
Chairman and Chief Executive Officer,
Consolidated-Bathurst Inc.,
Montreal, Quebec

VISCOUNT WEIR
Chairman,
The Weir Group Limited,
Glasgow, Scotland

DAVID WELHAM
Managing Director,
Royal Dutch/Shell Group of Companies,
London

SIR PHILIP WILKINSON
Deputy Chairman,
National Westminster Bank plc,
London

L. R. WILSON
President and Chief Executive Officer,
Redpath Industries Limited,
Toronto, Ontario

See footnote to statement

Author's Preface

When I wrote the preface to "The GATT Negotiations 1973-75: A Guide to the Issues", in February 1974, it was certainly not in my mind that many of those issues, hardly altered in form or substance, would still be the staple topics of negotiation in 1988. Much less could I have imagined that, fourteen years later, I should still find myself actively concerned in the international trade policy debate, or that my 1974 booklet would turn out to be the first of a series of which the present publication is the fourth.

I am, therefore, again grateful to the British-North American Committee for giving me this opportunity to continue the task which has emerged as the series progressed. This I have seen as twofold. First, I have tried to provide, even if in a necessarily summary way, a continuous record of the principal events and issues in the development of international commercial policy over the period from 1947 onward. Secondly, I have described the attitudes and approaches of the countries which have been the main participants in international trade and negotiation, and I have tried to offer an analysis of the issues. The first three booklets—The GATT Negotiations 1973-75: A Guide to the Issues; The GATT Negotiations 1973-79: "The Closing Stage"; and "Trade Issues in the Mid 1980s"—covered the period up to the eve of what turned out to be a somewhat ineffectual and disappointing Ministerial meeting of the GATT in November 1982. In this fourth booklet, I have discussed the aftermath of that meeting, the events which led to the meeting in Punta del Este in September 1986 and the inauguration of the Uruguay Round, and I have given an account of the negotiations which have since then been in progress in Geneva. Finally, I have attempted some assessment of the outlook for the "mid-term review" in Montreal in December 1988 and for the eventual outcome in 1990 (if the Uruguay Declaration timetable aspiration is achieved).

Recording the content and progress of the negotiations themselves has been enormously facilitated during the Uruguay Round, compared with its predecessors, by the excellent and commendably full and up-to-date information material which has been issued by the GATT Secretariat. But I have also to thank many friends in the GATT and other international organisations, both inside and outside government service, in London, Ottawa, Toronto, Washington, Paris, Brussels and Geneva, for the help and the pleasure I have had from my discussions with them.

It is a special pleasure to thank, for the fourth time, the BNAC for keeping up their interest in this subject (and for their publication of Sir James Ball's admirable essay on it[1]) and for their discussions of my

---

1 Ball, Sir James, *The Causes of Rising Protectionism,* BNARA, London, 1987.

preliminary papers at Eastbourne and Orlando in 1986 and at Gleneagles in 1987 (as well as for my great enjoyment at participation in those meetings). As always, I must particularly thank Simon Webley for his inexhaustible patience and generosity, and Norma Phoenix for coping courageously and uncomplainingly with my manuscripts.

As I have said in my previous prefaces, my intention throughout the series has been to analyse and inform rather than to make judgements. Insofar as judgements emerge, they are entirely my own, and not those of any of the people with whom I have had discussions or the BNAC.

SIDNEY GOLT
London
September 14, 1988

SIDNEY GOLT was formerly Advisor on Commercial Policy to the Board of Trade and a Deputy Secretary of the Department of Trade and Industry. He is now Advisor on International Commercial Policy to the International Chamber of Commerce, and a director of the international consultancy firm, Malmgren, Golt, Kingston and Co. Ltd.

CHAPTER I

The Uruguay Round

A meeting of Ministers of Trade of the countries which are
Contracting Parties of the General Agreement on Tariffs and Trade
(GATT) took place in Punta del Este, Uruguay, in September 1986.
The outcome of the meeting was the Uruguay Declaration, which
inaugurated a new "Round" of GATT negotiations. The "Uruguay
Round", the eighth in the series of multilateral trade negotiations, is
now in train in Geneva. The text of the Uruguay Declaration is
reprinted as Appendix 1.

The Declaration reads like a reasonably straightforward and
self-explanatory document. Its drafting was, however, the outcome of
a long and complex process of negotiation, going back many years,
and involving quite sharp conflicts of interest, and much sharper
conflicts of perception, among the participants about the conduct of
international trade. The starting point for the later stages of this
process may be taken to be the last Ministerial Session of the members
of the GATT, which took place in November 1982. That meeting,
it can now be seen, left undecided many difficult issues in the world
trade system; and the great majority of those issues, still undecided,
are now among matters committed to the Uruguay Round.

The problems of world trade policy and the stances of the principal
participants in the international debate, as things stood immediately
prior to the November 1982 meeting and the earlier history, are
described in detail in the previous publications in this series[1]. It may be
convenient, however, to provide a short summary of these background
events, as a basis for understanding the complex matters which are
now the substance of the Geneva negotiations, and for assessing the
machinery which has been established there and the tasks facing the
negotiators.

The next section of this study, therefore, is a short (and necessarily
summarized and simplified) account of what the GATT is, and how
it has developed over the 40 years since its inception, and an
explanation of the role of the successive Rounds of negotiations which
have taken place during this period.

---

1 The GATT Negotiations 1973-75: A Guide to the Issues (London,
 Washington, Toronto, British-North American Committee [BNAC], April 1974)
 The GATT Negotiations, 1973-79: The Closing Stage (London, Washington,
 Toronto: BNAC, May 1978)
 Trade Issues in the Mid 1980's (London, Washington, Toronto: BNAC,
 October 1982)

CHAPTER II

The GATT

Origins and Development

Those who shaped the international economic system and institutions after the Second World War were determined to try to avoid the mistakes which they saw as having been made in the prewar era and as having been among the causes of the war. A long process of debate and preliminary negotiations took place between the United States and the United Kingdom while the war was still in progress, and this was extended after the war to a wider group of countries. This culminated in the Havana Conference in November 1947, and the formulation of the Havana Charter. Unfortunately, the International Trade Organisation which the Charter envisaged never came into being, since the U.S. congress failed to rectify it, even though the U.S. Administration had been one of its principal architects.

Part of the preparation for the Havana Conference had included the drafting of an agreement on principles of international trade. This was brought into effect as the General Agreement on Tariffs and Trade on January 1, 1948. In the United States, the agreement was implemented without its having to be approved by Congress.

The GATT is a multilateral treaty to which more than 90 countries (a list is attached as Appendix 2), accounting for well over four-fifths of world trade, now subscribe. Its declared basic objective is to establish an open, liberal and competitive trading system so as to provide a framework of certainty and predictability about the conditions in which traders can conduct their transactions in the world's markets, and thus to contribute to economic growth and development, and to rising prosperity and welfare for the world's peoples. The Agreement is the only multilateral instrument that lays down agreed rules for the conduct of international trade.

Within these rules, the GATT also functions as the principal global body (as distinct from narrower regional or sectional bodies) concerned with negotiating progressive reductions of trade barriers and with international trade relations in general. The GATT is thus both a code of rules and a forum for negotiations.

The GATT was among the principal elements of the postwar economic institutional structure, the others being the International Monetary Fund (IMF) and the International Bank for Reconstruction and Development. It is worth remarking how we now take such international institutions for granted and forget what a truly revolutionary innovation they were. At first, only 23 countries were GATT members. Over the years, however, many other countries have joined, including many which had been colonies in 1947, and there are now 96 Contracting Parties. A further 28 countries have either acceded provisionally to the GATT or apply its rules to their trade without having formally done so.

The Agreement has not remained static during the 40 years of its existence. From time to time, there have been Review Sessions, some of which have resulted in modifications to a number of provisions, often in the form of interpretative notes annexed to the text. In 1965, following substantive negotiations, a new Part IV was added, dealing with the trade and development problems of developing countries. Throughout the whole period, however, developing country members of the GATT have been able to apply a number of its rules with considerable flexibility. Generally speaking, the GATT has been regarded as an adaptable instrument, which, for the most part, has facilitated a pragmatic accommodation of juridically binding obligations to politico-economic changes. These have included shifts in the relative economic strength of individual countries or groups of countries; the emergence of the Third World as a major factor in international affairs; the trend toward regional and, in some cases, preferential groups; monetary and balance-of-payment difficulties; and the increased participation of East European countries. These changes have imposed increasing strains on the fabric of the system, however, especially in recent years, and their effects have not been completely contained within it.

A Framework of Rules

The General Agreement is a long and complex document, but its basic principles and fundamental rules are relatively simple.

The central principle is that of nondiscrimination among trading partners—the so-called most-favoured-nation (MFN) clause. This principle has had a long history, far predating the GATT, in bilateral international trade treaties. The innovation of the GATT was to multilaterise it. Under the MFN clause, all contracting parties are obliged to grant to all other members of the Agreement treatment as favourable, in relation to their trade policies, as they give to any other country; no country's traders are to be given more favourable treatment than those of any other member country. So, in particular, if a customs duty is reduced as a result of negotiation with one country, it must similarly and automatically be reduced for all member countries without further negotiations with any of them. The Agreement allows exceptions to this rule only in special circumstances.

The MFN does not prohibit favourable treatment for a country's own producers against foreign suppliers. However the GATT's second basic principle is that if such favourable treatment is given—that is, if a country wishes to accord "protection" to its domestic producers—it may do so only by the use of the customs tariff, and not in any other way. In all other respects, foreign suppliers are to be treated the same as nationals—that is, given "national treatment". The objective is to ensure that all suppliers can trade with clear knowledge of the trading conditions—free from arbitrary and unpredictable intervention— and thus to make competition possible, subject only to known tariffs. In addition, these tariffs are subject to negotiation, and thus to progressive mutual reduction and "binding" — that is, undertakings not to increase them above the levels arrived at by negotiation.

GATT members can depart from the MFN rule if (i) a number of them are prepared to enter into a customs union with each other or, under fairly stringent conditions, to form a free trade area; or (ii) if a country operates a scheme for preferential tariffs in favour of developing countries. A special Article in the Agreement covers the first of these circumstances. The second is provided for by procedures under which the Contracting Parties, acting together, can grant "waivers" which allow members to derogate from particular GATT obligations. This waiver procedure is also available to allow countries to seek such derogations if special economic or trade circumstances warrant them; but it has, naturally, been used rather sparingly.

These principles, allied with the general rule that members should exercise the greatest possible use of the consultation and dispute settlement procedures established in the Agreement, constitute the core of the GATT. The rest of the Agreement is directed almost entirely toward ensuring that members do not indulge in practices which would undermine or circumvent the basic rules. The principal provision of this kind is the general prohibition of quantitative restrictions. In the 1930s, these became a widespread method of protection—much more rigorous, arbitrary and destructive than the tariff — and were used even more prolifically at the end of the Second World War. A prime objective of the creators of the GATT was to end the use of quantitative restrictions as instruments of protection, both because they were destructive of international trade and because they were an obvious method of circumventing agreements reached on tariff bindings. The GATT's creators accepted, however, that there might be a case for the use of such restrictions when a country was in severe balance-of-payment difficulties, and even on a discriminatory basis against imports from a country whose currency was "scarce". It was under those provisions that most countries continued for many years to limit imports from the United States.

Other GATT rules, including those on export subsidies and dumping, on the use of internal taxes and regulations and on the way in which state-owned commercial enterprises should conduct their trading, are designed to the same end—to produce conditions of open and equal competitive trading between suppliers from other member countries, subject to only the known rate of tariff protection, if any.

All this said, however, the Agreement's creators still recognised that the complexities of the world trading system might need some safety valves, and that some flexibility had to be built into the system. There are, therefore, provisions for a number of general exceptions to the rules—on grounds of national security, for example, and a few other exceptional circumstances. But there is also a special Article—Article XIX, on "safeguards"—which, under certain conditions and with rights of redress for the exporter, permits a member country to impose restrictions or to increase a bound tariff on imports in order to prevent or to limit "serious injury" to domestic producers. Article XIX, sometimes by its use, but more often because the conditions it imposes on such safeguard actions have been bypassed or circumvented, has now become perhaps the most controversial and intractable element in the commercial policy debate.

It will be seen from this much condensed account that the GATT is far from being a monolithic and doctrinaire monument of "free trade" dogma. On the contrary, it has proved to be an adaptable and flexible system. It is, however, because of this very flexibility, which has been used so permissively, that the discipline of its basic principles has now been put in jeopardy.

CHAPTER III

GATT Negotiations: "The Rounds"

"The substantial reductions of tariffs and other barriers to trade" was laid down as a principal aim of the GATT at the beginning, and has been pursued as the objective of a long series of trade negotiations. There were six "Rounds" (as they came to be called) of negotiations in the first 20 years of the GATT: in 1947 (Geneva), 1949 (Annecy), 1951 (Torquay), 1956 (Geneva), 1960-61 (Geneva—the "Dillion" Round), and 1964-67 (Geneva—the "Kennedy" Round). Additional smaller-scale negotiations preceded the accession of particular countries (for example, Japan, Switzerland, Hungary) to the Agreement. As a result, the tariff rates for thousands of items entering world trade—which, at the outset of the process, had stood at very high levels—were reduced or "bound" against increase. The peak of the process was achieved in the Kennedy Round, as a result of which the average level of world tariffs was reduced by about one-third. By the time these reductions had been implemented fully (they were brought into effect by stages), customs duties, in the major industrial countries at any rate, were no longer a major obstacle to world trade.

The magnitude of this outcome was in large part the consequence of the most-favoured-nation rule. The early (and, as will have been noticed, commendably rapid) Rounds were, in essence, large-scale tariff negotiations among the major trading countries (though a number of smaller ones also participated), and were usually on a bilateral basis with the "principal supplier" of the product under negotiation. The technical innovation the GATT provided was to bring all its contracting parties together and engage them in the negotiations, still on a bilateral basis but in the same place and at the same time, instead of on a piecemeal, individual and isolated basis. The effect of the MFN rule then meant that the results of all the separate bilateral negotiations were generalized and made available to all other GATT countries. The average level of tariffs on industrial products in the major industrial countries thus was brought down to about 13 percent by the early 1960s and to around 4 percent by 1986.

In some respects, the very success of this process has created, or at least contributed to, the problems of international trade policy since the beginning of the 1970s. With tariffs no longer a major inhibitor of trade, surviving nontariff barriers have become more visible, more significant and more irritating. The emphasis of the debate focused on the comparatively small, hard core of obstinately remaining import and quota restrictions, as well as customs valuation methods, administrative and procedural restrictions on the movement of goods, the potential use of technical standards to give advantage to domestic products, the growing significance of government procurement (which

6

had not been covered effectively in the General Agreement), and other less easily recognisable and more indirect obstacles. Almost without noticing it, the Rounds have undergone a substantial change in character. In the Kennedy Round to a small extent, but much more clearly and insistently in the Tokyo Round (1973-79) which followed it, these more difficult and complex matters took over from tariffs as the topics for negotiation. There was still some negotiation on tariffs, by no means unimportant, in the Tokyo Round. But by far and away most of the time was spent on these non-tariff matters.

The difficulty and complexity of negotiating on these topics, compared with tariff negotiations, is compounded in two ways. First, tariff negotiations can be conducted on a more or less quantifiable basis. The quantifications may be rough and ready, and sometimes perhaps intellectually dubious. But they do at least provide some basis for assessing an "equivalence" of concessions on each side, and for measuring the significance of the bargain being struck. Negotiations on non-tariff barriers are, in general, much more about concepts and conduct than about quantities. Second, they usually cannot be reduced to bilateral bargaining and then generalized. The debate, by its nature, is multilateral from the beginning and thus is much more difficult to manage.

The negotiating Rounds thus have now taken on a new form. They have become opportunities for GATT countries to review together, in a continuous and intensive operation, the whole range of trade rules, to consult with all their trading partners on the concerns and trade objectives of each of them and to try to assemble a package of results which will provide a balanced outcome of some advantage and benefit to each participant.

Inevitably, a Round of this kind is bound to take longer than did the simpler, earlier Rounds. The Tokyo Round, which was the first to be engaged fully in this way, lasted for six years—although it should be noted that serious negotiations were not possible for much of this period because of extraneous circumstances in both the United States and the European Community. In the end, the Tokyo Round produced, in addition to its tariff-reducing content, a substantial package of agreements on a wide variety of subjects—technical standards, government procurement, subsidies, antidumping, customs valuation, import-licensing procedures, safeguards and dispute settlement. Much of this outcome was embodied in "Codes" which, although supplementary to the GATT, did not become a substantive part of the General Agreement. They were set as as separate instruments which each country was free to accept or stand aside from. In the event, most of the industrialised countries have subscribed to the Codes, but the developing countries have been much less willing to do so. (Appendix 3 presents the current situation on adherence to the Codes.)

CHAPTER IV
International Trade in a Changing World

The GATT's 30th birthday took place during the Tokyo Round, and a major effort was made to tackle some of the problems this passage of time had brought to the surface. On some matters, the agreements which came out of the Tokyo Round worked well and made effective improvements in the system. On others, however, it soon became clear that the agreements, and the "Codes" which were based on those agreements, were at best only partial answers to the problems. In some cases—including the most difficult areas, such as subsidies and safeguards—they rested on exhortation and the hope of goodwill, rather than on firm commitments and obligations, or they simply transmitted the unsolved problems to a process of further negotiation as a continuing task within the standing consultation procedures of the GATT.

The conclusion of the Tokyo Round did engender some guarded optimism for further international cooperation in the field of commercial policy. But the outcome of the Tokyo Round did not really remove the worries and tensions in international commercial relations which had made its decisions necessary. We can, indeed, now see with hindsight that the Tokyo Round did not come to grips with the structural changes which had already taken place in the world economy by the beginning of the 1970s.

The most important of these was, in fact, quite outside the GATT's own field of competence. The international exchange-rate system had rested effectively on the relationship of all other currencies to a firm and stable U.S. dollar, and on a substantially stable pattern of relative rates among the other major currencies. This key element of international relationships was weakened dramatically when the United States cut the formal link between the dollar and gold in August 1971. It is not an exaggeration to say that the shocks to the system resulting from this action, which, in effect, meant the breakdown of the post war IMF exchange rate system, have still not been cured, even in the late 1980s. There have been considerable efforts to provide a more effective co-ordination of the policies of the major monetary countries, and some progress has been made. But the world has not yet achieved a really adequate way to deal with the interrelationship of trade and monetary movements. This has become all the more difficult to achieve with the vastly increased volume of financial movements across frontiers. Exchange rate volatility is now a significantly unsettling factor in the conduct of international trade.

This has been the most visible manifestation of the changes in international economic relationships in the period since 1945. And the scale and pace of change have gone on increasing throughout the 1970s and 1980s. At the outset of the period, the financial, industrial and trading power of the United States was dominant, as supplier, as market, as source of capital and of technology, for every other trading country in the world. But first the rehabilitation of Europe and then, much more significantly (and traumatically), the emergence of Japan as a formidable, and seemingly uncontainable, industrial force and commercial competitior have radically altered the world scene. Instead of the comparatively simple pattern of the immediate post war period, there are now three more or less equal major trading powers, in competition and often in conflict with each other, as well as many smaller countries with substantial economic trading power. There is thus a vast network of economic relationships of immense complexity.

This means that many more countries now play a significant part in world trade, and their actions and policies may have a substantial effect in an increasing number of sectors. It can no longer be assumed, as it was in the 1950s and 1960s, that a comparatively small number of countries, on the whole like-minded on trade policy, conduct the vast majority of the world's trade. Equally, of course, the smaller countries—especially when they can act in concert—now have a larger voice than they had in the affairs of the international organisations. And the potential economic and commercial significance of this greater number of players on the world scene is enhanced immensely by the much greater scope for technology transfer and the ease of capital investment.

Finally, communications and transportation technologies have outgrown dramatically the evolution of political organisations. Real economic interdependence has increased in such a way that policies which were formerly matters of internal domestic interest often now have a worldwide impact on trade patterns. Again, the significance of this change is multiplied by the great extent to which governments have increased their interventions in industrial and commercial activity in the pursuit of national economic objectives. It is the interaction of these developments which has produced some of the sharpest international conflicts, and has created intractable difficulties in relations among the major industrialised countries, and between them and some of the leading developing countries.

In the face of these changes in the structure of the world economy and in the relative positions of the participants in world trade, a substantial erosion of the international trade system took place. The Tokyo Round and its immediate aftermath only partially and temporarily halted this erosion. By mid-1981, a widespread feeling had developed that if the system were to survive, some new and strong political commitment on the part of governments to its maintenance and improvement was essential. In November of that year, it was agreed that the 1982 annual Session of the GATT Contracting Parties should be held at the Ministerial level, and that it should address the problems affecting the functioning of the multilateral trading system. Its objective was to reinforce "the common efforts of the contracting parties to support and improve the system for the benefit of all nations."

The approach to the 1982 Ministerial Session and the problems it had to face were examined in detail in *Trade Issues in the Mid 1980s*, which was published in October 1982, immediately before the meeting took place. That examination ended by looking back to the closing passages of the two preceding studies in the series. It noted the progressively increasing fears about the erosion and weakening of the international trading system, coupled with the hope that governments everywhere, especially in the major countries, would recognise the dangers inherent in the policies they were pursuing and would, in good time, set in train a reversal of the trend toward protectionism. The 1982 publication ended with the following paragraph:

> If the 1978 conclusion was more pessimistic than that of 1974, it is difficult, in July 1982, to find now much new ground for optimism. What one can say, however, is that in spite of everything the GATT does survive still, and that governments do still feel it necessary to re-assert their adherence to it. If the present discontents can be surmounted, the 1982 Ministerial Meeting can even now make its contribution to the reversal of the drift into bitter trade war between the major trading powers, with the consequences that would bring for all the countries of the world. But it will be the actions and policies of Governments over the next years which will decide this outcome, not the minutiae of the communique from Geneva at the end of the 38th Session (held at Ministerial level) of the Contracting Parties to the GATT.

CHAPTER V

Towards the Uruguay Round, 1982-86

In the event, the 38th Session's Ministerial Meeting did not resolve any of the problems, and produced little more than a work program for trade policy officials in their national capitals and in Geneva and for the GATT Secretariat. The matters to be covered were defined on much the same lines that had been forecast: the unfinished work of the Tokyo Round, especially safeguards; agriculture; review of the Tokyo Round codes; nontariff obstacles in general; and dispute settlement. There was a tentative reference to some preliminary fact finding on trade in services, but no commitment to substantive discussion. This was accompanied, as had been expected, by a suitably pious reaffirmation of devotion to the principles of the GATT and the liberal trading system. But it was apparent to even the most casual observer of the trade policy scene that virtually nothing of substance had been achieved, and that there were not likley to be any rapid changes of significance in national policies, especially those of the United States and the European Community, which, together with Japan, are bound to be the main determinants of the patterns of world trade.

The working parties and committees set up in the GATT after the November 1982 meeting had been charged to report to the 1984 session, and they continued to work, with measured deliberation, for the next two years. On most subjects, it continued to be clear that nothing new was emerging. Somewhat surprisingly, it seemed at one time possible that the Agriculture Committee might produce something near to agreed recommendations, which, if implemented, would have done quite a lot to restore some discipline of international rules to world trade in agricultural products. This prospect was soon dispelled, however, by the unwillingness of the European Community to endorse it. Meanwhile, the United States intensified its trend toward negotiating bilateral restrictions on imports, through voluntary export restraints or other forms of managed trade, in a number of individual sectors—outstandingly steel, but others, including automobiles and electronics, as well. The European Community acted similarly, especially in relation to Japan. It was apparent that neither major trading power was inclined to change its attitude significantly on textile imports from developing country producers. There was also a general hardening toward the newly industrialising countries, which were becoming more substantial participants in world trade in a still comparatively narrow, but continuously widening, range of manufactured goods. At the same time, there was increasing acrimony in relations between the United States and the European Community, especially over agricultural subsidies and exports.

An important element in the situation during this whole period was the general economic policy of the United States and its effects on the world economy. Demand expansion encouraged by substantial budget deficits, an overvalued dollar sustained by high interest rates and a massive inward flow of money—which, astonishingly, turned the United States into the world's largest debtor and capital importer—produced, *inter alia,* a substantial and continuously increasing visible trade deficit. This no doubt contributed to a welcome, if precarious, growth in general world economic activity, but it fuelled dangerously the growth of U.S. protectionist sentiment and pressures from domestic industrial interests. Protectionist forces in the U.S. Congress gathered strength from these events; and the Administration, though often acting courageously in the face of severe pressure, was, on balance, forced to give ground.

Slowly, against this background, there emerged the belief in some quarters that to institute a new major Round of GATT negotiations, which was to concern itself primarily not with tariffs but with the general problems of the system, was the only way to try to ameliorate the situation. The U.S. Administration, in the hope that a new Round would help it domestically, was the principal advocate of this. But the whole process of discussion on it was still characterised by lack of clarity about objectives, by the patent divisions and dissensions between the major protagonists and by the reluctance of the developing countries, led by India and Brazil, to seem to allow themselves to be pressured by the United States. There was also a nagging feeling that there was little point—and a good deal of hypocrisy—in a formal Round to discuss strengthening and extending the GATT in new areas, such as services, when the troubles arose from the clear unwillingness, or inability, of the major countries to live up to their professed attachment to liberal trade and to abide by existing rules of the GATT in the areas to which it already applied.

In November 1983, GATT's Director-General, Arthur Dunkel, on his own initiative, tried to break through what he saw as the rigidity and increasing deterioration of the situation by inviting a group of seven eminent independent persons to make a study of the problems and to make recommendations to governments for their improvement. The member governments showed little enthusiasm for Mr. Dunkel's initiative, but they did not actually veto it. The group, under the chairmanship of Fritz Leutwiler, published its Report in February 1985 (its recommendation are in Appendix 4). It included a number of recommendations for urgent action, as well as longer-term ones; and it endorsed the need for a new Round of negotiations—the sooner the better. What the group wanted from this was a bold, fresh look; it believed that a new Round still held the seeds of hope for a "better future for all the world's people," as an alternative to "escalating troubles and, eventually, disaster."

Although there was no very visible sign that governments had read the Leutwiler Report, let alone taken much note of it, the idea of holding a new Round, in the hope that it would put a break on deterioration and eventually rehabilitate the system, gradually secured the support of both Japan and the European Community, and the effort to launch it began to be put in train. But the hopes that had been expressed in both 1984 and 1985, that the formal autumn Session of the Contracting Parties would define the terms and operations of such a Round and set a date for its commencement were still frustrated. As late as July 1985, Brazil and India, with support from some other developing countries, remained strongly opposed. It was only by a majority vote—virtually unprecedented in GATT procedure on such matters—in September 1985 that a Preparatory Committee was set up with the remit to prepare the agenda and modalities of a Round and to report to a Ministerial meeting to be held in September 1986.

CHAPTER VI

The Preparatory Committee, 1985-86

Even in this closing stage of the preliminary discussions, doubts about the Round, and especially about its scope and purpose, persisted. On the one side were those—almost entirely the industrialised countries—who felt that what was needed was to deal with the fundamental problem of bringing the GATT up to date. In particular, they saw it as an opportunity, given the changes in world economic patterns and the growth in interdependence, to extend the principles of GATT application and practices to aspects and areas where they had not originally—especially to trade in services, now visibly more important in the economies and trade of many countries. For others, including many of the influential developing countries, it seemed more important to restore and secure proper implementation of obligations in the areas already covered before more ambitious projects, and especially extensions to new areas, could expect to carry any credibility. For them, the priority was to foster a "standstill"—that is, to stop the major industrialised countries from creating new restrictions—and to start reviewing and trying to "roll back" restrictive measures which had proliferated over recent years.

The debate throughout the spring and summer of 1986 continued to be uneasy and sometimes turbulent. To some extent, of course, the participants were staking out negotiating positions for the Round itself. The United States language about the importance of including services and improving the defence of intellectual property rights became even more strident: Clayton Yeutter, the U.S. Special Trade Representative, talked at one time about the readiness of the United States to "walk away" from the negotiations and, by implication, to desert the GATT system altogether. The European Community insisted that in no circumstances could the negotiations impair its Common Agricultural Policy. Brazil and India continued to deny the GATT mandate to be involved in negotiations about services.

Meanwhile, other related events in Geneva and elsewhere added further complexities to the situation. The long standing but still troublesome international arrangements about the organization of international trade in textiles embodied in the Multifibre Arrangement (MFA) were due to expire on July 31, 1986, and negotiations about its future were concurrently in progress in Geneva. The arrangements were a potential source of rancour between industrialised and developing countries. In addition, however, if some revised agreements could not be reached in time, there might have been other difficult consequences, especially in terms of action by the U.S. Congress. In the event, an eleventh-hour agreement was achieved, under which the MFA was extended for a further period, from August 1, 1986, to July 31, 1991.

So another difficult hurdle on the path to a new Round had been surmounted. But this had not been done without a fair amount of acrimony on both sides. The importing industrialised countries accepted, as part of the new Protocol, that the final objective must be the reapplication of GATT rules to trade in textiles. The exporters, however, did not secure a firm commitment that this would necessarily be the last extension of the MFA. The exporters were also obliged to accept that a number of fibres not previously covered by the MFA might be brought within its scope. Throughout, the possibility that the overall situation might be irrevocably soured by new protectionist legislation in the United States remained an overhanging factor. The U.S. Administration continued to denounce any legislation on the lines of the bill which was then before the House of Representatives as contrary to the interests of the United States and certain to incur a presidential veto. But this could not dispel the general feeling that whatever U.S. legislation eventually was enacted, it would be detrimental in some respects to prospects for the liberal trading system.

Dissensions between the United States and the European Community over such items as pasta, citrus fruit and steel also simmered on through the summer. The two sides struck a temporary truce, giving a further six months for discussions before mutually retaliatory actions were undertaken, in the argument over the effect on U.S. trade of Spanish and Portuguese accession to the Community; but other issues remained unsettled. Indeed, new causes of dissension emerged, notably the potential consequence for Europe of agreements between the United States and Japan. The U.S.-Japanese agreement on semiconductor trade and prices looked to the Europeans suspiciously like a bilateral and discriminatory deal on the organisation of world markets, and on the pattern of future world location of manufacturing plants.

In these circumstances, it was not surprising that the Preparatory Committee failed to agree on a draft to be submitted to the Ministerial Meeting that was to be held in Punta del Este, Uruguay. Three alternative versions, in fact, were put forward. It was fairly clear, however, that one of these — a draft sponsored by Switzerland and Columbia, which eventually secured support from about forty countries—would be the basic working document. It still contained many disputed passages, but it did begin to look like a possible first draft of a "declaration" to emerge from the Punta del Este Session of the Contracting Parties. Even so, a last-minute bout of French intransigence on agriculture meant that the European Community was unable to endorse it; and it seemed not at all impossible that the Punta del Este Session might be troubled by the same internal Community stalemate that had done much to stultify the GATT Ministerial session in 1982.

The Preparatory Committee completed its work on July 31, 1986, but two other events of interest took place between then and the opening of the Punta del Este Session of September 15. What may turn out in the long term to have been the most important of these events was the emergence of a new grouping of countries crossing the divide between developed and developing. On August 25-27, a meeting of Ministers from 14 countries calling themselves "Fair Traders in Agriculture" convened in Cairns, Australia, under the leadership of Mr. Hawke, the Australian Prime Minister. The "Cairns Group"—Argentina, Australia, Brazil, Canada, Chile, Columbia, Fiji, Hungary, Indonesia, Malaysia, the Philippines, New Zealand, Thailand and Uruguay—agreed on a Declaration which was, in effect, a strong denunciation of the agricultural policies of the European Community, Japan and the United States, and they established themselves as a continuing alliance on the agriculture issue for the duration of the Uruguay Round. (The text, and Mr. Hawke's keynote remarks, are attached as Appendix 5.)

A development of a rather different character was the Soviet Union's intimation of its interest in taking part in the new Round of negotiations and of possible membership, or at least some form of participation, in the GATT. This met with a cool response from both the United States and the European Community. Equally cool was their reaction to a suggestion from Nigeria that South Africa should be excluded from the Uruguay Round.

Sparring continued into the Ministerial Session itself. It was eventually brought to an end only by the text which was finally produced in Punta del Este on September 20. Of course, all those involved hailed the outcome as an historic achievement. To the extent that the session escaped the disaster of breaking up in complete disarray—with indeed the United States' walking away from GATT and the consequent collapse of the post-1945 international trading system—that assessment is perhaps justified. But the content of the Uruguay Declaration and of the Punta del Este outcome needs to be examined in more detail. And, as always, it will be possible to make a proper and balanced assessment only when we see the actual effects on the policies and conduct of governments in the years ahead.

CHAPTER VII

The Uruguay Declaration, 1986

The events leading up to the eventual promulgation of the Uruguay Declaration have been spelt out here partly to maintain the continuity of the narrative which was begun in the first publication in this series, *The GATT Negotiations, 1973-75*, and continued in its two successors. Taken together, this study and its predecessors give a concise account of the whole process of trade policy negotiations during the postwar period. More important, perhaps, is the fact that without some knowledge of the course of these events, it is difficult to understand the differing approaches of the main participants in the negotiations, or the inwardness of the language of the Declaration. For the same reasons, a few general comments are needed on the actual drafting of the Declaration before turning to a more detailed analysis of its individual topics. In a number of cases, the drafting skillfully papers over, or conceals, the real differences among participants, which made the process of achieving, first, the holding of a Round at all, and second, the definition of its terms of reference, so long and tedious.

First, it must be appreciated that although matters of real and important substance lay below the attitudes taken by the participants, the long debates preceding the setting up of the Preparatory Committee, in the Preparatory Committee and in the Ministerial Session itself were entirely about procedure. The Declaration, with a few exceptions, leaves all the matters of substance, and even some important matters of procedure, still open to the whole negotiating process. As an outstanding example, the entire argument about agricultural export subsidies was not about whether and how they should be brought to an end, or about what rules should be applied to them, but simply about whether these matters should be discussed at all. On the main matters at issue, there were virtually no negotiations of substance.

Secondly, however, it must be recognised and acknowledged that much of the general language of the agreed text, as well as some of the detail, does represent a significant achievement of international co-operation, given the difficult atmosphere and attitudes toward international trade liberalization characteristic of the mid-1980s, compared with what these were even at the time of the Tokyo Declaration in 1972. The preamble and statement of objectives of the Uruguay Declaration provide a robust re-statement of liberal trade principles and political commitment to the GATT. They are also more explicit about the "linkage between trade, money, finance and development" than are most previous international pronouncements. They specifically include, as an objective of the negotiations, the need to "foster concurrent co-operative action at the national and international levels to strengthen the inter-relationship between trade policies and other economic policies affecting growth and development." This perhaps can be taken as an implicit recognition that many aspects of a country's internal domestic policies have significant consequences for its international trade patterns and those of its trading partners. However, the Declaration stops well short of any explicit recognition of such interdependence, except, as we shall see later, in relation to agriculture. In parallel with this, there is a high degree of commitment to international surveillance procedures and to the improvement of existing surveillance and dispute settlement methods. But the drafting does not indicate any readiness to widen the field for surveillance beyond what are strictly "trade" measures. There is no evident concession to the rather wider horizons of the Leutwiler Report.

There are three topics on which the Declaration particularly reflects the conflicts of attitude among the participants: the service industries, agriculture and "standstill" and "rollback".

The issue of the service industries was, of course, the hardest dividing line between many developing countries and, primarily, the United States—which, however, received the full support of the European Community and Japan. The United States wanted to have services fully integrated into the entirety of the negotiations. Brazil, India and others wanted to see the GATT play no part in services (if, indeed, there were to be services negotiations at all). The working draft included a square-bracketed passage which called for negotiations on services, but said that "when the framework of principles and rules has been established", the Contracting Parties should decide "regarding its incorporation in the GATT system".

The Declaration treats the whole question differently. The Declaration is, in fact, in two separate Parts, and there is an esoteric, but extremely significant, difference in drafting between them. Part I is recorded as a decision of the CONTRACTING PARTIES, (in the conventional, binding GATT form); and deals specifically and exclusively with trade in goods. Part II pointedly departs from reference to the CONTRACTING PARTIES, and says simply that "Ministers also decided, as part of the Multilateral Trade Negotiations, to launch negotiations on trade in services". For this purpose, a separate Group of Negotiations on Services was to be established; but it would also eventually report to the central Trade Negotiations Committee.

This tortuous and potentially contentious drafting went far enough to satisfy the United States, even though the Director-General of the

GATT confirmed that it meant that the services negotiations were not "placed under the legal framework of the GATT". It did at least get the discussion about a system of rules for services in train at last, and it also specified that "GATT procedures and practices" shall apply to the negotiations. But it certainly established a separate track for the services negotiations. This may not be wrong; but it is not what the United States set out to achieve. Any agreement of substance on rules for services will, in any case, and whatever the formalities, take a very long time indeed.

The second issue, almost equally significant and controversial, is agriculture. The Tokyo Round, and the Kennedy Round before it, began with vehement protestations from the United States that agriculture must be a central element in the final settlement. In each case, little emerged. It must be supposed that this time things will be different. One new feature is the existence of the group of agricultural countries referred to above as a continuing, organised force. Another is the growing public recognition of the enormity of the distortion in world trade and in domestic economies, too, that current agricultural policies create. This applies especially in the industralised countries, but it is, in fact, a world-wide phenomenon.

The European Community eventually agreed to a formulation on agriculture in the Declaration which is significantly wider than that contained in the working draft which it would not endorse. The Declaration specifies the need to "bring all measures affecting import access and export competition under strengthened and more operationally effective GATT rules and disciplines", and to improve the competitive environment "by increasing discipline on the use of all direct and indirect subsidies and other measures affecting directly or indirectly agricultural trade, including the phased reduction of their negative effects and dealing with their causes".

It may be cynical to suggest that a field of negotiations as wide and drafting as ambigious as this offers a fair chance that any substantial outcome can be long delayed. Certainly, the formulation has achieved the European Community's objective of ensuring that its Common Agricultural Policy will not be the only target of discussion.

The third issue is the question of standstill and rollback. The inclusion of provisions on these was virtually a sticking point requirement for the leading developing countries. This was particularly the case for the newly industralising countries, which have seen progressively increasing restrictions—violations, in their view, of both the spirit and the letter of the GATT—imposed on their growing exports. In the event, the Declaration's paragraphs dealing with standstill and rollback are, unlike the rest of the Declaration, substantive commitments which were to commence "immediately"; they are not merely rules of procedure. On the face of it, proper observance of them could bring about an important change in the whole atmosphere of international trade relations. But a careful reading of the language used throws considerable doubt on the likelihood of this outcome. The standstill commitment is specifically limited to "any trade restrictive or distorting measure inconsistent with the provisions of the General Agreement or the Instruments negotiated within the framework of GATT or under its auspices". Both the United States and the European Community made it very clear that they accepted this language as meaning that they are under no obligation to eschew the use of many—if indeed, any—of the various restrictive devices which have grown up. They will continue to argue that these measures are outside the GATT and not inconsistent with it. Indeed, it is already apparent from some of the actions of both the United States and the European Community that the standstill provision is unlikely to bring about any significant change in their conduct of trade policy. Implementation of the rollback provision seems even more precarious, since it depends on the establishment— presumably by negotiation—of an "agreed timeframe not later than by the date of the formal completion of the negotiations."

These commitments were made "subject to multilateral surveillance", and a Surveillance Committee was established, which will make "periodic reviews and evaluations". These will no doubt be read with interest not only as reports on the progress of standstill and rollback themselves, but as indications of the credibility and viability of the whole process of the Round.

Finally, comment must be made on an item which was not formally part of the Declaration and which attracted little public attention, but which, in the light of events since Punta del Este, may prove to be indicative of an important element in the development of international trade policy. In recent years, the European Community increasingly has put great stress on the question of "imbalance and disequilibrium" in its trade with Japan. The Community pressed hard to have something about this specifically mentioned in the Declaration. For once, the Japanese, who have habitually played their hand very quietly, reached strongly against what they regarded as "Japan bashing", and denounced it as contrary to the multilateral and nondiscriminatory character of the GATT; and they secured a good deal of support. In the event, the Community had to be satisfied with a statement by the chairman of the session, which summarised the discussion which had taken place and was issued together with the Declaration, but not as part of it. This statement, again clearly carefully drafted, recorded the opposing views without referring to particular countries. It conceded that growing disequilibrium constituted a serious problem, but saw the remedy as going much beyond trade policy. It stopped well short of endorsing the kind of bilateral reciprocity which the Community seemed to be pursuing, or of accepting that this was a matter to be pursued in the Round. (The text of this statement is reproduced in Appendix 6.)

CHAPTER VIII

Starting the Uruguay Round

The Uruguay Declaration was signed on September 19, 1986. The negotiations machinery it established consisted of a Trade Negotiations Committee, with a general supervisory role, and under its two negotiating "groups": the Group of Negotiations on Goods (GNG) and the Group of Negotiations on Services(GNS). No remit was defined for the GNS. The GNG, however, was instructed to work out detailed negotiating plans, to establish subgroups as required and to co-ordinate their work, as well as to designate mechanisms for the surveillance of standstill and rollback commitments.

Work on setting up this machinery went on through the autumn, with the Director-General of the GATT taking the chair of both the Trade Negotiations Committee and the GNG, and Ambassador Felipe Jaramillo of Columbia the chair of the GNS. On January 28, 1987, the negotiating plans were agreed. The GNG set up 14 groups, one for each of the topics mentioned in the Declaration, and the GNS adopted a programme for the initial phase of the negotiations on trade in services. The Trade Negotiations Committee endorsed these decisions, as well as the agreed mechanism and procedures to carry forward the negotiations. A list of the negotiating groups, and their chairmen, is found in Appendix 7. The final drafts of the basic guidance documents for the negotiations — the surveillance mechanism, the decisions on negotiating structure and the negotiating plans — are found in Appendix 8.

CHAPTER IX

Topics for Negotiation

We now turn to considering in more detail the topics which are the main subject for negotiations during the Uruguay Round, looking at what is known of the stances of the principal participants, and what has happened so far in the negotiating groups, and, so far as is possible, assessing the prospects for the negotiating outcome. Some topics, inevitably, call for more extensive treatment than others.

The most convenient way to deal with these topics is to comment one by one on the important items as they appear in the Declaration, and to give an account of what has happened in the negotiations so far. On some topics, the main participants have tabled at least their initial positions and proposals. On others, they have still to declare themselves, and their likely stances have to be inferred from other sources. We shall, therefore, look in turn at the following:

- standstill and rollback;
- tariffs;
- non-tariff measures;
- agriculture;
- safeguards;
- subsidies and countervailing measures;
- tropical products, natural resource-based products and textiles;
- intellectual property rights and trade-related investment measures;
- trade in services; and
- dispute settlement and the functioning of the GATT system.

These sections cover all the negotiating groups except the two which are concerned with a general review of GATT Articles and with a similar review of the Tokyo Round Codes not dealt with by other specific groups. The work of these two groups may well raise interesting questions, and even some important ones; but they are largely technical and specialist in character, and it is unlikely that any of them will be crucial to the outcome of the negotiations.

The discussion of these topics is followed by a section on the effort—which the United States strongly advocates—to produce an "early harvest" of results. This effort has led to agreement that there be a "mid-term" review meeting of Ministers in Montreal in December 1988. Finally, there is a concluding section on some background factors and on the prospects for the future.

Standstill and Rollback

The Declaration's inclusion of provisions explicitly requiring a standstill on measures in contravention of GATT rules and the rollback of such measures already in operation was in itself a clear indication of the deterioration of the disciplines of the international trade system. There were no such provisions in the Tokyo Declaration of 1972, presumably because at that time there was no strongly felt need for them. Their inclusion as a formal undertaking at Punta del Este was a gesture to the force of the feeling, especially among developing countries, that the erosion and disregard of existing GATT rules had to be halted for the Round to have any chance of success, or even credibility. It was, indeed, the least that had to be done if the principles of the GATT were to be extended to new areas or given wider application.

Substantive action under the provisions is, of course, for the countries concerned. However, the Declaration also called for the establishment of surveillance machinery to operate under the Trade Negotiations Committee. The Surveillance Body which was established considers "notifications" by any participating counties about practices to which either the standstill or rollback provisions are relevant. During its meetings in 1987 and the first half of 1988, specific notifications were made about a score or so different practices. Nearly one half were about U.S. practices, ranging from discriminatory action against Swedish speciality steels, through the doubling of tariffs on some Japanese electronic exports, and to various manifestations of the "Buy America" program. Many of the rest were about practices of the European Community. In every case, the country complained against defended its actions. The United States, for example, claimed that the Swedes had failed to observe voluntary export restraints that other countries had accepted, and that the Japanese were not complying with a bilateral restraint agreement. There is no indication that any country has changed any of its practices, except for the single case of Greece's lifting an import ban on almonds. The United States has reduced some of the offending tariffs on Japan, but this was clearly in response to their damaging effects on U.S. industry, not because of international pressures.

There have been general discussions about the significance of the rollback provisions, but no rollback measures have so far been put into effect. The European Community has offered to eliminate over 100 quantitative restrictions covering a variety of products; but it has made this conditional on "similar contributions from other participants", and some exporting countries—including, to some extent, Japan—have been excluded from benefiting from the offer.

The Surveillance Body reported, as required, to the Trade Negotiations Committee at the end of 1987. The Committee apparently simply took note of what had happened without substantive debate. For the time being, we must expect the Surveillance Body to continue operating on much the same lines as it has so far. Sooner or later, however, more searching questions about the value of the Uruguay Declaration provision are bound to be raised. The mid-term review will be the first occasion on which serious misgivings—already aired within the Surveillance Body by Canada and Australia—will have to be addressed by the main particpants at the Ministerial level.

Tariffs

The Uruguay Declaration calls for "negotiations . . . to reduce or, as appropriate, eliminate tariffs including the reduction or elimination of high tariffs and tariff escalation", with emphasis on "the expansion of the scope of tariff concessions among all participants."

The Negotiating Group on Tariffs began by asking participants to submit proposals on tariff cutting methods, appropriate areas for elimination or reduction of high tariffs and tariff escalation—that is, the increased effective level of protection resulting from applying higher tariffs according to the degree of processing— and criteria for expanding tariff bindings. The aim is to establish a common negotiating basis on these issues, with bilateral negotiations between participants on particular items, to produce, in total, a package of agreements for multilateral implementation.

Tariff reduction in itself is not the first priority of the Uruguay Round. However, the Negotiating Group's discussions so far show that there are still a number of aspects of the use of customs duties which are of considerable importance, and which will give rise to negotiations of some substance.

The elements at issue are somewhat different from the earlier Rounds. Up to and including the Tokyo Round, the main objective was to reduce substantially the general level of tariffs of the major industrialised countries; in the Tokyo Round, this was achieved by agreement on a general formula. What is now generally accepted to be at stake, as far as the major countries are concerned in their relations with each other, is the comparatively small number of tariff rates—the surviving "peaks"—which are "significantly in excess of the average level of tariffs maintained by most of the developed trading nations" (to quote an early European Community definition of its objective). This time, on the other hand, both the Community and the United States—again by contrast with earlier Rounds—would like to discuss the level of tariffs of some of the smaller countries, especially those which are now highly competitive in world markets for some manufacturers, but which continue to maintain exaggeratedly high tariff protection in their own markets, and whose tariffs, for the most part, are not subject to bindings.

Altogether more radical proposals were put forward quite early, by the Japanese. These called for total reductions to zero for the tariffs of all developed countries, except for agriculture, fisheries, mineral and forestry products. They also called for the developing countries to begin applying bindings to a proportion of their trade, the bound share increasing according to the degree of development. Neither the United States nor the European Community has shown any indication to move so far. Nor has either country shown any inclination to accept a Brazilian proposal, which other developing countries support, that the industralised countries eliminate *all* their duties, in the first place for ten years for the developing countries, and thereafter for all participants, with the developing countries "considering" binding some of their tariffs and, possibly, after the ten-year period, making reductions.

In this whole area, then, there are no serious conflicts between the Europeans and the Americans, although there are differences, partly of emphasis, between their proposals. The European Community proposes a combination of approaches to narrow the gap between what it describes as the "levels of obligations" of different participants. There should be a general formula for reducing high tariffs and an increase in bindings by countries that have not already accepted such bindings. For industrial goods with tariffs in the medium range, the Community would like to see a request-and-offer procedure of the traditional type, while low tariffs would be candidates for further reduction only on a case-by-case basis. Tariffs on tropical products, agriculture and natural resource-based products would be considered separately (in the Negotiating Groups concerned with them). The whole system would be conditional on a general undertaking by all participants to achieve full binding of industrial tariffs, and on the condition that tariff reductions should not exacerbate existing imbalances.

The European Community's proposals are clearly aimed at trying to impose some discipline on the virtually uncontrolled tariff regimes of the developing countries, especially those such as Brazil and South Korea, which play an increasing (and already substantial) role in world export trade, but which have not correspondingly modified their own tariff systems. (Hong Kong, by contrast, would have little to worry about in these proposals, since it has virtually no import duties at all).

The United States' proposals have not gone anything like as far as those of the European Community to date. It has suggested that the developed countries be subject to a request-and-offer procedure on tariff peaks and escalation, with additional negotiations on particular sectoral issues. For other countries, there would be a general formula for across-the-board reductions. However, general U.S. statements about the tariff regimes of countries such as South Korea imply that the United States would certainly not dissent from the European Community's objectives, if they were attainable.

The United States has also tried to push the idea of an integrated approach to the tariff negotiations which would see tariff and non-tariff barriers as a combined pool for consideration under a request-and-offer system. This has found support from Canada and Australia but not from the European Community, and it has been generally unacceptable to the developing countries as well.

Much of the substance of these proposals, and of others which are on the table, may have been overtaken by a detailed programme for an across-the-board tariff cutting formula put forward by a group of seven countries: Australia, Canada, Hong Kong,, Hungary, South Korea, Switzerland and New Zealand. Under this plan, a base rate for the negotiations would be calculated; broadly speaking, this would be either the most-favoured-nation bound rate of January 1, 1988, or if there is no binding, the MFN rate normally applicable either at that date or the date of the Uruguay Declaration. The formula, which is designed to bear more sharply on high than on low tariffs, would be applied to all goods without exception. The resulting levels would then be bound by all countries, including the developing countries, although the plan includes some special treatment for them—a longer transition period, and a more favourable adaptation of the formula.

It may be recalled that a formula approach, proposed by Switzerland, was part of the final settlement in the Tokyo Round (its mechanism and effect is described in detail in the second paper in this series, *The GATT Negotiations 1973-79: The Closing Stage, p.19).* It was, however, accompanied by a good deal of negotiation about the treatment of specific items which one country or another did not wish to subject to the automatic discipline of the formula. There was still a good deal of traditional request-and-offer negotiation.

It seems probable that some of this same process will happen again in the Uruguay Round, although the joint proposal does seem to go some way to meeting the concerns of a number of different groups. Whatever detailed course the negotiations may take from now on, however, they are bound to concentrate on the main substantive issues. These are the desirability of removing the highest peaks in the developed countries' tariffs on industrialised goods, the effects of tariff escalation on developing countries' exports and the need at least to begin to introduce some bindings—and in some extreme cases some reductions—into the tariff systems of the most advanced developing countries. There are not likely to be significant conflicts among the major countries (although there may be quite sharp negotiations on one of two items). It will still be necessary to find some way to secure progress by countries such as Brazil and South Korea which will satisfy the European Community, and that will not exacerbate the general debate between developed and developing countries. (The Brazilians have indeed said that "changes in their customs system" will lead to a significant reduction of their tariff average. Australia, too, has reported a phased tariff reduction programme.) At the end of the day, there may be some subtle bargaining between the outcome here and what happens in other areas of the negotiations, especially, perhaps, on the safeguard provisions. The joint proposal has already explicity linked the tariff negotiation process to progress in the other Negotiating Groups.

Nontariff Measures

The decision to have a separate Negotiating Group to deal with "nontariff measures" is to a large extent a hangover from traditional GATT practice. During the Tokyo Round, the phrase was used as a general catch-all description of any form of government intervention, other than the tariff, which affected international trade. The illustrative list drawn up by the GATT at the time was organised under five headings: "government participation in trade" (which included, *inter alia,* export subsidies, countervailing duties, government procurement and state-trading); "customs and administrative entry procedures" (including valuation, anti-dumping rules and customs classification and formalities); "standards"; "specific limitations on trade" (including quantitative restrictions and export restraints, minimum price regulations and some other miscellanea); and "charges on imports" (including prior deposits, variable levies and discriminatory taxes on motor cars). Many of these items eventually were dealt with in the Tokyo Round by the creation of separate Codes, and will be considered in the Uruguay Round in the context of the review of those Codes by a Negotiating Group charged specifically with this task. Some of the topics—outstandingly, subsidies—have separate Negotiating Groups allotted to them. Others will be looked at in the Negotiating Group which has been given the task of a general review of the Articles, provisions and disciplines of the GATT. Finally, several measures and practices will clearly have to be examined in the Negotiating Group on Safeguards.

It is not surprising, therefore, that the discussions that have taken place in the Negotiating Group whose aim it is to "reduce or eliminate non-tariff measures" have been somewhat amorphous and inconclusive. The main line of division seems to have been between the supporters (a few developed countries) and the opponents of the U.S. proposal that the group adopt a "market access" approach by considering all "market impediments" as eligible for request-and-offer negotiations. Both tariff and nontariff items could be brought into the pool of negotiations. The developing countries clearly believe that this would be the start of a process requiring them to make concessions in return for the abandonment of practices they consider to contravene the GATT.

The European Community appears to have suggested a different approach, one which would attempt to evaluate practices so as to assess whether they would be amenable to multilateral action or be better dealt with bilaterally. The Community wanted the group to refrain from dealing with matters covered by other Negotiating Groups—as we have seen, a pretty severe limitation—and perhaps to concentrate on measures not covered by the GATT as it exists. Items so identified would be listed in a "Central Negotiating Register". This suggestion, like that of the United States, has not yet commanded general support.

So far, therefore, this Negotiating Group has not really found its role. Until more progress is made in the other groups whose subject matters overlap with it, it seems unlikely to make a significant contribution to the eventual outcome of the Round.

Agriculture

The Uruguay Declaration's text on Agriculture is very broad indeed. It covers, as matters relevant to the negotiations, virtually all forms of government policy toward agriculture, including all domestic subsidies and other kinds of domestic intervention, as well as export subsidies. It talks of the urgent need to bring more discipline and predictability to world agricultural trade, to deal with distortions and structural surpluses, to achieve greater trade liberalisation and to bring "all measures affecting import access and export competition under strengthened and more operationally effective GATT rules and disciplines". It spells out in quite considerable detail how it sees these results being achieved: by reducing import barriers, by improving the competitive environment through disciplining the use of all direct and indirect subsidies and other measures affecting agricultural trade, directly or indirectly, "including the phased reduction of their negative effects and dealing with their causes"—it was the inclusion of this phase which enabled the Community to accept the text—and by minimising the adverse effects that "sanitary and phytosanitary" regulations and barriers can have on trade.

The Negotiating Group on Agriculture defined the initial phase of its work as essentially a far-reaching fact-finding exercise: the identification of "major problems and their causes" and the elaboration of "an indicative list of issues considered relevant by participants", together with "full notification of all . . . subsidies and other measures affecting . . . agricultural trade". There would also be "consideration of basic principles to govern world trade in agriculture". The subsequent negotiating process would aim to agree on:

    (a) comprehensive texts of strengthened and more operationally effective GATT rules and disciplines; (b) the nature and the content of specific multilateral commitments to be undertaken including, as appropriate, implementation programmes and transitional arrangements; (c) any other understandings which should also be deemed necessary for the fulfilment of the Negotiating Objective; and (d) exchange of concessions, as appropriate.

On the fact-finding side, much work had already been done in the GATT Committee on Trade in Agriculture following the 1982 Ministerial meeting, but this will no doubt need updating, and much of 1987 was taken up in pursuing these exercises (which are, indeed, still continuing). Beyond this, the objectives are no doubt unexceptionable. If they are achieved, not only will agricultural trade be transformed, but a revolution in the whole pattern of international trade relations will have taken place.

This is, however, the area of the most intense international conflict, and the strongest and most deeply entrenched domestic vested interests. The broad and bland texts of the Declaration and the Negotiating Group mask the bitter conflict between the United States and the European Community about their respective agricultural regimes and, in particular, about the use of both domestic and export subsidies. They also understate the strength of feeling among the traditional agricultural exporters, led by Australia and Canada, about the aggressive encouragement of agricultural production, including the creating of unmanageable surpluses, by the United States and the European Community, as well as the less-publicised but equally strong resentment, especially in the United States, about Japan's virtually prohibitive agricultural tariffs.

All these cross currents of interests are reflected in the various proposals that have been put forward in the Negotiating Group. Among the major countries, the United States has tabled the most radical proposals, covering all agricultural commodities, food, beverages, forest products and fish and fish products. These contain three main elements. First it proposes a complete phase-out, over ten years, of all agriculture subsidies which affect trade and a freeze on export subsidies; there would be exceptions, however, for direct income or other payments not related to production and marketing—this is, income support schemes like those the United Kingdom used before joining the Community. Second, it suggests the elimination of import barriers over ten years. Third, it would like to see harmonisation of health and sanitary regulations.

Negotiations, according to the U.S. plan, would go ahead on two levels. On one, there would be agreement on a method of measuring aggregate support to agricultural products from all forms of government aid. Much work has already been done in the Organisation for Economic Co-operation and Developments (OECD) in devising such a measure—know as the "Producer Subsidy Equivalent" (PSE)—and this could be used in the negotiations. The objective, on this level, would be a schedule for progressive reduction of PSEs to zero. The second level of negotiations would aim at identifying and agreeing on specific policy changes needed to get countries to commit to reduce their overall support systems. The ten-year implementation plan would rank as a binding of PSE levels. The negotiations would also have to put in place appropriate GATT rules to cover agricultural trade after the ten-year transition period.

The reactions to these far-ranging U.S. ideas were predictably cautious. Even the Australians felt they needed time to consider the wide range of products covered, and that harmonization of health and sanitary regulations was a bit beyond the negotiating mandate of the Declaration. The most openly hostile were, uncharacteristically, the Japanese, who voiced precisely the opposite philosophy: the need to treat agriculture differently from other sectors, to preserve national self-sufficiency for security reasons and not to be over ambitious in liberalisation aspirations, even as a starting point for negotiations.

Japan's own proposal rested on these considerations, and asserted a claim to be "realistic". The Japanese accepted a freeze (as an emergency measure) on export subsidies, followed by their gradual elimination and a "strengthening of discipline" on other trade-distorting subsidies. But they saw a continuing and justifiable case for a wide range of permissible domestic subsidies as an integral element in national agricultural policies. Specifically, they rejected the relevance or value of the PSE, or any other measure of comprehensive aggregate support, to the Uruguay Round negotiations; such a measure, in their view, could not reflect the wide-ranging purposes of policy. Nor did they see any need to treat negotiations on agriculture as more urgent than other elements of the entire Round. The Japanese have seldom put forward proposals of their own in so decisive and uncompromising a form, and this must signal the strength of their desire to maintain both their agricultural policies and as much as they possibly can of the protection they give to their producers.

The European Community's proposals eschew both the radical reforming fervour of the Americans, and the overt self-sufficiency philosophy of the Japanese. However, they clearly rest on a strong reluctance to relinquish the principles, and a good deal of the current practice, of the Common Agricultural Policy. They were put forward as being pragmatic proposals designed to deal with the situation as it exists, recognising that national support measures have had damaging effects on international markets. Accordingly, they suggest a two-stage approach. The first stage would be based on existing policies, modified to put in place emergency measures, covering the cereals, sugar and dairy products sectors. These would consist chiefly of a year of disciplines and measures to reduce quantities put on the market with the possibility of renewal if this was not long enough. Participants would also undertake to reduce internal and external support measures so as to prevent the exacerbation of existing imbalances. The second stage, even less clearly defined, would aim at measures to reverse the trend towards structural disequilibria and permanent instability. It would involve the gradual replacement of production support by income support and the renegotiation of external protection. Perhaps by its tone, as well as by the vagueness of its formulation, the Community's submission gave the impression of a distinct lack of enthusiasm for substantial reform of the system and, in particular, a surviving intention to retain the possibility of the right to subsidise exports.

The Cairns Group originally put forward strong proposals for early action on agriculture, which it sees as a "down-payment" on long-term reform. Such short-term action, it says—and this is the Group's criticism of the Community's proposals—should be "directly linked to and consistent with long-term reform". What the group wants is a freeze in the 1989-90 crop year, and the beginning of reductions in global support for agriculture, and in production and export subsidies, as well as immediate increases in access opportunities and agreement on the management of surpluses. It also wants a firm commitment on the elements of a long-term framework of rules, particularly on the elimination of both domestic and export subsidies and other import restrictions inconsistent with GATT principles.

More recently, the Cairns Group has made a brave attempt to bring together the U.S. and European Community approaches by offering what it hopes will become the first draft of a mid-term progress report. Initially, both Americans and Europeans saw this attempt as a helpful contribution, and gave it a moderately friendly reception. But neither of them offered any endorsement of the Cairns Group's proposals. It soon became clear that the United States thought that the Group, by dropping any time limit on the elimination of subsidies, had gone much too far toward trying to satisfy the European Community, while the Community was still unwilling to accept any such commitment even without a time limit. The Japanese, too, regarded the liberalisation aspirations as overambitious.

The Negotiating Group on Agriculture thus has a formidable task on its hands. Notwithstanding the Cairns Group's efforts, the positions taken by the participants, as outlined above—and there are also others, particularly from developing countries, claiming various kinds of privileged treatment—do not lend themselves easily to compromise. Moreover, the views they embody reflect strongly held objectives of national policies and the concerns of powerful domestic interest groups. The United States, in spite of significant declines in its agricultural exports in the 1980s, is still the world's most important agricultural exporter. Pressure for agricultural trade reform has been put at the forefront of the United States' negotiating strategy. The Cairns Group, for whose members greater freedom of agricultural trade is central to their economies, will also continue to exercise great pressure.

It must be remembered, however, that repeated efforts to restore international discipline to agriculture—which, unhappily, was first breached by the waiver granted to the United States over 30 years ago—have, equally repeatedly, run into the sands of the negotiating process. Whether this happens again in the Uruguay Round may well depend less on the negotiations themselves than on the development of domestic opinion, policies and pressures over the next two or three years, particularly in Europe. Europe's agricultural problems—which are of peculiar political complexity—are even more related to relations among the member states of the Community, and to conflicting interests of different groups within the states (farmers versus the rest), than they are to conflicts with the outside world. There is, indeed, increasing awareness of the damaging effects on taxpayers, on consumers, and on the community's economies as a whole of some aspects of the Common Agricultural Policy. But Community governments do not yet seem ready to make the radical changes which are necessary to reverse this situation. Their most recent decisions on agriculture, reached only after the most difficult and painful negotiations, have introduced some elements of improvement. But these have come only at the cost of entrenching the system as a whole and making it improbable that much more drastic changes will be agreed to within the projected time span of the Uruguay Round. We have to expect that the Community's tactics in the Round are bound to include persistent delaying of any general subjection of agriculture to the rules of the GATT. In this stance, it will no doubt be discreetly, but stubbornly, supported by Japan, which, in spite of its agricultural protectionism, is still the world's largest importer of agricultural products, and will be reluctant to offer significant concessions.

If this clear divide on agriculture were to lead to only insignificant improvement, through very limited agreement, in the situation, how serious would this be for the negotiations as a whole? It would, of course, produce severe (and justified) resentment by Canada, Australia, New Zealand and the other countries of the Cairns Group. But the United States was just as insistent about the importance of agriculture at the outset of the Tokyo Round, and in the end quietly swallowed that Round's meagre outcome. It is probably much less likely that this could happen a second time, but the possibility of its doing so will not be entirely absent as a factor in the negotiations.

All this said, there is, no doubt, a growing feeling throughout the world that the burdens of existing agricultural policies in many countries are inflicting a great deal of damage on national economies and the global economy in general. It must be supposed that, sooner or later, common sense will break through, but the outcome of the Toronto Economic Summit in June 1988 is a clear indication that the time for this has not yet arrived.

Safeguards

The debate on the use of "safeguard" measures as a means of additional protection for industries under special threat from imports was the principal, and most apparent, unfinished business of the Tokyo Round. It was, similarly, unfinished business of the November 1982 Ministerial Session, and the continued extended debate inside the GATT failed to produce any result. It is this unresolved difficulty, indeed, which is at the heart of the malaise of the international trading system.

The Uruguay Declaration asserted that:

a comprehensive agreement on safeguards is of particular importance to the strengthening of the GATT system and to progress in the [negotiations, and that this agreement]:

- shall be based on the basic principles of the General Agreement;
- shall contain, *inter alia*, the following elements: transparency, coverage, objective criteria for action including the concept of serious injury or threat thereof, temporary nature, degressivity and structural adjustment, compensation and retaliation, notifications, consultation, multilateral surveillance and dispute settlement; and
- shall clarify and reinforce the disciplines of the General Agreement and should apply to all contracting parties.

The Negotiating Group on Safeguards added nothing of substance to this in defining its work programme. Participants were asked to put forward their suggestions for achieving the negotiating objective in this area, and the Secretariat was instructed to prepare a paper on the work already done in the GATT. This simply meant resuming a debate that has gone on for more than a decade now.

The nub of the problem is left completely unstated in both the Declaration and the mandate of the Negotiating Group. The real difficulty lies in the fact that GATT Article XIX, on safeguards, requires that actions are to be taken only on a nondiscriminatory basis, while all the pressures to use such measures are to do this by restricting imports from the particular source, or sources, seen to be responsible for the difficulty. As long ago as 1974, the first publication in this series, *The GATT Negotiations, 1973-75*, defined the issue as follows:

Industrial opinion in most countries which have been the recipients of those imports held to cause the 'injury' has moved toward arguing that this [that is, selective action] is the only logical, and likely to be the only effective, course. But many . . . governments . . . would be very unwilling to see a formally approved breach of the most-favoured-nation principle, and would argue that this would undermine many other elements of the General Agreement.

Nothing in essence has changed since then, except that there has been a vast proliferation of discriminatory schemes—the whole bandwagon of "grey-area" measures of voluntary export restraints, orderly marketing arrangements, inter-industry agreements on market sharing and so on.

The discussions that have taken place in the Negotiating Group have done little, if anything, to carry the debate significantly further forward. The United States and the European Community have not so far tabled formal proposals. However, the United States seems likely to favour an attempt to bridge the gap by providing a "two track" procedure. In effect, this would legitimise grey-area measures, provided they were arrived at by agreement between the parties concerned, were duly notified, and did not damage other member countries. The Community has not specifically endorsed this approach, but has said that there should be an effort to find "a broader understanding" on the safeguards issue, including the possibility of selective action.

The main formal submissions to the Negotiating Group of substance have so far come from Brazil and India. There have also been submissions from a number of other developing countries, and from the Scandinavians. All, except the Scandinavians, who avoid the selectivity issue, emphasise and re-affirm the principle of nondiscrimination. The Brazilian proposal is that countries should legitimately take only two kinds of measures in response to damage to domestic industries attributed to imports: domestic adjustment assistance and import relief, to be secured only by an increase of tariffs on an MFN basis. Such tariff increases would be permissible, moreover, only after determination by an international surveillance body that there existed "persistent" serious injury, and they would be exercisable for a fixed number of years. On this basis, all grey-area measures and quantitative restrictions in pursurance of Article XIX of the GATT would be ended, and the restrictions permitted under the Multi-fibre Agreement would be phased out.

The reactions from the major countries to these proposals, and to much vaguer and more general suggestions coming from a group of Pacific Rim countries (Australia, Hong Kong, South Korea, New

Zealand and Singapore), and to the well argued and more modest Indian submission, have been predictably cautious. The general concepts of temporariness, degressivity and transparency are given a broad degree of acceptance. The United States and Japan, however, have emphasised the need for "pragmatism" in their application, and the European Community has made no secret of its view that selectivity in some form cannot, in the last resort, be avoided. All in all, the Negotiating Group seems to be covering the same debating ground that was trodden so thoroughly by the negotiations in the Tokyo Round and in the GATT discussions leading up to the 1982 Ministerial Sessions and since.

At the end of the day, it needs to be recognised that the recourse to safeguard measures over recent years is a symptom of the failure of the industralised countries to accommodate to changes in world circumstances and patterns; and that only fundamental structural adjustment will really put an end to, or at least mitigate, the problem. What is needed, in fact, is a radical change of attitudes, rather than a simple revision of texts. In an expanding industrial and trading world, in which there was an improved atmosphere of trade relations between established and new competitors and greater readiness for change in the older economies, the safeguards issue and its protectionist consequences might be much less abrasive. Without such progress, the Uruguay Round may well end as indecisively on this issue as did its predecessors.

Subsidies and Countervailing Measures
The Uruguay Declaration picked out subsidies and countervailing measures as a specific topic for a separate Negotiating Group. The remit to the group was that "negotiations on subsidies and countervailing measures shall be based on a review of Articles VI and XVI [of the GATT] and the [Tokyo Round] Agreement, with the objective of "improving GATT disciplines relating to all subsidies and countervailing measures that affect international trade". The Negotiating Group has not tried to spell this out in more detail, but has simply asked participants to submit proposals, and the Secretariat to prepare factual background information and analysis.

The provisions of both the GATT and the Tokyo Round Code on the use of subsidies, and on the circumstances in which it is legitimate for an importing country to impose countervailing duties against goods which it regards as benefiting from subsidy, are still not very precise, and consequently are capable of giving rise to differences to interpretation and to international conflict. The most frequent and bitterest source of such conflict is in relation to agricultural products; but these agricultural aspects of subsidy are to be dealt with primarily as part of the negotiations in the group on agriculture—although the results there eventually will have to be related back to the outcome in the subsidies group.

Subsidies and countervailing duties were regarded as almost the most important and troublesome area of the Tokyo Round negotiations. This was, perhaps, for two special reasons. The first related to countervail, and particularly to the position of the United States in this respect. That country, as a legacy of history—because of the way in which the GATT originally came into being and because of pre-existing U.S. legislation—had not been subject to the GATT limitation, which other countries accepted, that the imposition of countervailing duties required prior demonstration of injury, or threat of injury, to a domestic industry. The second was that the 1970s—the period of the Tokyo Round negotiations—was when governments tended most to use interventionist "industrial policies", with subsidization of industrial production as one of the principal tools, to try to direct and organise the pattern of industrial development in their countries. Inevitably, such subsidisation—especially when it became competitive between countries—distorted, and sometimes (as in the case of shipbuilding) virtually destroyed, normal market conditions.

There was not, and still is not, dissent among the major trading countries about the basic concepts involved. There was, and is, general acceptance of the proposition that exports of manufactured goods should not be directly subsidized, and that such subsidization provides, in principle and subject to certain rules, a *prima facie* case for the importing country to countervail. The difficulty arises in trying to determine whether exported goods which have benefited from domestic subsidies—sometimes perhaps quite indirectly, as, for example, from using subsidized components or other inputs—might also legitimately be countervailed. On this issue, there was a considerable difference of emphasis during the Tokyo Round between the United States and the European Community; this still persists.

The outcome of the Tokyo Round left this difference of emphasis unresolved. The Subsidies Code went far enough to enable the U.S. Administration to accept, and to secure legislative approval for, the "injury" condition for countervailing measures. It also provided rather more substantial procedures for conciliation, consultation and disputes, and it exhorted participants to refrain from using domestic subsidies in ways which would damage the interests of their trading partners. It did nothing, however, to clarify or identify the sort of subsidies which might have this effect. Indeed, by giving explicit approval to the concept of the use of subsidies for a number of purposes of national policy, it appeared to have weakened rather than strengthened the already ambivalent existing GATT rules. It was, therefore, an open question whether the Tokyo Round outcome would significantly affect government policies in this area.

As things have turned out, it is now fairly well evident that the Code has had little influence on governments, and that when they have wished to use subsidies as an instrument of industrial policy, the Code has not significantly inhibited them from doing so. It was, therefore natural that the subject should still be on the agenda, and the differences in attitude between the United States and the European Community persist.

The United States has put forward its views in a submission which presses for review and strengthening of the Subsidies Code. The European Community's first concern—and that of a number of other countries—clearly is to try to secure greater clarification on the use of countervailing measures. The Community has said in the debates in the group that regional subventions to industry and subsidies for structural adjustment purposes on inputs should not be regarded as subsidies to international trade. Canada has been generally inclined to support the U.S. view.

A more substantive formal proposal has been put forward by Switzerland, and this may now focus the debate more sharply. The Swiss have gone back to the attempt made, under U.S. pressure, during the Tokyo Round, to categorise subsidies according to their degree of acceptability and relevance to international trade, rather than their ostensible domestic purposes. They propose three groups: practices which would be prohibited outright; practices which would be "actionable", by which they mean subject to countervailing or other forms of retaliation; and "non-actionable" practices, which would be accepted as legitimate and not subject to any kind of international counter-actions.

Clearly, if progress on these lines were achieveable—which has not been the case in earlier negotiations—a considerable advance would have been made. It is perhaps possible that something might be done this time, in a general political atmosphere which has moved a long way from the pervasive interventionism of the 1970s. But it is still difficult to foresee the creation, without considerable technical and drafting difficulty, either of formulae which would fit the categories proposed or of lists of specific practices which would command general agreement.

It may well be that the general trend of policy in this area—always, of course, excepting agriculture and food products—has taken, and will continue to take, some of the heat out of the issue. With very few exceptions, subsidised exports of manufactured goods are not currently a major cause of dissension among the major countries. There will, no doubt, be some pressure, especially from the United States, on some of the advanced developing countries. But the issue is not likely to become—as at one time seemed likely during the Tokyo Round—central or crucial for the overall outcome of the Round.

Tropical Products, Natural Resource-Based Products and Textiles
It is convenient to group these items together because, in one way or another, they are matters of central interest to developing countries, and the manner in which they are dealt with will be one of the main touchstones by which those countries will assess the outcome of the negotiations. They are not areas where there will be substantial conflicts of interest among the major countries, except to the extent that there may be some measure of competition among them to earn credit with the developing countries.

On tropical products, the Uruguay Declaration said that the negotiations should aim at the fullest liberalisation of trade, including trade in their processed and semiprocessed forms, and should cover both tariffs and nontariff measures. It also implied that the special attention given to the topic might result in early implementation of any agreement on it.

The progress of the work in the Negotiating Group seems to be living up to these professions. There seems already to have been a fair degree of agreement on the products to be covered, and the group is the first to have laid out a timetable for negotiations on substance to be completed—this, at least, is the aspiration—by the end of 1988. The European Community has made substantial proposals for the elimination or substantial reduction of both tariffs and other restrictive measures over a very large part—although, to the disappointment of some producing countries, not quite all—of the range of products. However, the Community has accompanied its offer by quite stiff conditions about what it would expect other countries—including the centrally planned economies—to contribute. These include a "fair" degree of "burden sharing" by other developed countries, some reciprocity, in the form of acceptance of obligations, by the more advanced developing countries and reductions in restrictions on export by countries, including developing countries, that have a dominant position as suppliers. The United States, on the other hand, initially caused some disappointment by seeking to link any progress in this field too closely to the negotiations on agriculture generally but now seems willing to modify this position.

Generally speaking there seems so far to be a spirit of reasonable optimism that, by contrast with earlier rounds, and especially the Tokyo Round when little was achieved in spite of special discussions on the issue, there may well be something useful, and even something expeditious, this time. There will, of course, be even more acute and troublesome disappointment if these high hopes are not realised.

The inclusion of natural resource based products as a separate negotiating topic has always been something of an enigma. It seems to have originated in U.S. feelings that producers were imposing unfair restrictions on access to supplies. The Declaration said that the negotiations should aim to achieve the fullest liberalization of trade in natural resource-based products, including their processed and semiprocessed forms, and to reduce or eliminate tariff and nontariff measures, including tariff escalation.

The discussions that have taken place in the Negotiating Group so far have been very much in the realm of generalities, with the United States and the European Community reciting what they see as difficulties besetting trade in these products. These include dual pricing, export restrictions, subsidies, government ownership and export taxes, as well as tariffs and nontariff measures. Developing country producers have so far taken the line that the developed countries are pitching the agenda for discussions far too wide, and in some respects well outside the GATT's field of competence. It is not yet clear how successful this Negotiating Group can be at finding a basis for fruitful talks, especially as much of the material which can be brought strictly within the GATT's area cannot easily be separated out, for this rather specialised sector, from its discussion as part of the work of other functional Negotiating Groups. It may be well into 1989 before the likely outcome of this work can be discerned.

The establishment of a special Negotiating Group for textiles and clothing was clearly inescapable, given their importance for the developing countries and the history of the treatment of textile imports by the major trading countries. The Declaration calls for the negotiations to aim to formulate modalities that would permit the eventual integration of this sector into the GATT on the basis of strengthened rules and disciplines, "thereby also contributing to the objective of further liberalisation of trade".

Not unexpectedly, the pace of negotiation in this area has been far from hasty. The year 1987 was spent virtually entirely in updating or preparing new documentation; international trade in textiles must now be about the most thoroughly documented trade topic in the world. Beyond this, there have been little more than doctrinal re-statements of existing positions, and neither the United States nor the European Community has in any way indicated any intention of refraining from further attempts to renegotiate the Multifibre Agreement when its present period expires in 1991. On the contrary, the United States has talked about liberalisation "within existing agreements".

Here again, there is no division of interest among the major trading countries. There may well be quite considerable conflicts, however, which have not so far come to the surface, among the developing country producers. The MFA protects not only inefficient producers in the importing countries. It also shelters, to a considerable degree, inefficient producers in some developing countries by guaranteeing them a share of the markets which they could lose to more efficient competitiors if indeed textile trade were "re-integrated" into the GATT system and the MFA were scrapped.

The negotiating course in this group, therefore, must be expected to be tortuous and slow. And the eventual outcome may be influenced by general factors in world development patterns as much as by negotiations in the group. The general patterns and growth of world trade as a whole, and changes in the production and export trade of the more advanced developing countries—Hong Kong, South Korea, Taiwan, India, Brazil and others—may have significant effects by the time the Uruguay Round negotiations draw to a close.

Trade Related Aspects of Intellectual Property Rights and Investment Measures

The trade-related aspects and effects of intellectual property rights (TRIPS) and of governmental measures dealing with investment (TRIMS) are "new" to the GATT in the sense that they have not been the subjects of negotiations in any previous GATT Round, although both topics have been discussed within the GATT, and a surprisingly large number of GATT Articles can be shown to be relevant to them. The most substantive previous discussions in the intellectual property area have been about trade in counterfeit goods. These were, indeed, carried to the point of drawing up and circulating, in 1982, a Draft Agreement on Measures to Discourage the Importation of Counterfeit Goods, but no further action was taken on it.

The pressure to include these topics as integral to the Uruguay Round negotiations came first—and for some time only—from the United States. There is now general support from most of the developed countries, more, perhaps for TRIPS than for TRIMS. Some developing countries may also be beginning to accept the inclusion of TRIPS but most, including some of the leading ones, are still luke-warm at best about the GATT's becoming deeply involved in these issues. There are, however, differences in attitude and in interests between the two topics, and they are, of course, being dealt with in separate Negotiating Groups.

On TRIPS, the agreed text of the Uruguay Declaration said that:

> In order to reduce [obstacles] to international trade, and taking into account the need to promote effective and adequate protection of intellectual property rights, and to ensure that measures and procedures to enforce intellectual property rights do not themselves become barriers to legitimate trade, the negotiations shall aim to clarify GATT

provisions and elaborate as appropriate new rules and disciplines. Negotiations shall aim to develop . . . principles, rules and disciplines dealing with international trade in counterfeit goods. These negotiations shall be without prejudice to other complementary initiatives that may be taken in the World Intellectual Property Organisation and elsewhere to deal with these matters.

As can be seen, this was a very carefully negotiated text, reflecting both the objectives of the United States and some of the concerns some countries felt about extending the GATT's role in this area, and about potential threats to their own interests. It foreshadowed the kind of discussion that has since gone on in the Negotiating Group.

The work of the group began with analyses from the United States, Japan and the European Community, which set out what they saw as the problems in the existing situation and which tried to convince the other participants that these were indeed trade problems which should be tackled inside the GATT and as part of the Round. The analyses referred to discrepancies in national laws—in some cases none, in others inadequate; insufficient protection of rights pertaining to patents, trade marks, designs and copyrights; and inadequate intellectual protection with regard to new technologies such as computer software, semiconductor chips and biotechnology. All these, the analyses argued, hindered legitimate trade and were disadvantageous both to the owners of the intellectual property affected and to countries that failed to benefit from its use.

These arguments failed to receive any enthusiastic response, but the United States followed up with a formal submission setting out a comprehensive negotiating plan. This proposed a GATT intellectual property agreement to reduce distortions and impediments to trade caused by deficient levels of protection and inadequate enforcement of intellectual property rights. The agreement, the United States argued, should set out minimum standards which would be the norms on which to base national legislation, and it would be implemented by internal enforcement measures at the national level and through GATT consultation and dispute settlement procedures. The European Community supplemented this by proposals which aimed to secure protection for intellectual property both internally and at the frontier, with customs administrations playing a more active part in checking counterfeiting, and equality before the law for foreign owners of intellectual property.

Initially, developing countries were highly sceptical and unreceptive to these initiatives, and they continued to emphasize the view that all the proposals went far beyond the mandate of the Declaration and the competence of the GATT. Some countries, however, seem to have moved part way to accepting discussion of some—but still strictly limited—trade-related aspects of these topics, although without commitment.

On this issue, then, the differences are not among the major developed countries, but between them and the great majority of the developing countries. The United States, Japan, the European Community and most other OECD countries would have little, if any, difficulty in reaching agreement. But this in itself would have little additional value for those countries unless at least some of the main developing countries could be induced to come aboard. The discussions of substance are, of course, still at an early stage. Indeed, the developing countries still feel that the secretariat needs to do a good deal of fact finding and analysis. If there is to be any positive outcome in which the developing countries eventually participate, it is not likely to come about until a good deal later in the negotiating process.

On TRIMS, the Declaration was much terser, and even less committal. It called for an "examination of the operation of GATT Articles related to the trade restrictive and distorting effects of investment measures," following which, "negotiations should elaborate, as appropriate, further provisions that may be necessary to avoid such adverse effects on trade." This cautious language clearly signaled that this was indeed a "new" subject for GATT negotiation and that, in traditional GATT fashion, the first steps would require a substantial fact-finding and information-collecting process by the Secretariat. This process had not been completed by the end of 1987, and continued into 1988.

The Negotiating Group's discussions, meanwhile, have gone barely beyond procedural questions. Attempts by the United States and Japan and, somewhat less insistently, the European Community to open up questions of substance have achieved little response, A submission from Malaysia however, indicates some modest interest in the issues by the developing countries, subject, as always, to their insistence on special treatment. A number of U.S. case studies purporting to demonstrate the distorting effects of various investment measures—especially requirements about local content and export performance as a condition of permission to make investments in production—have served simply to evoke the familiar argument that investment policy is a central facet of sovereignty and of the right of governments to control and direct the pattern of individual and economic development, and that it is no business of the GATT to meddle in the matter.

So far, then, no commonality of views has been achieved. And here again, it can only be in the later stages of the negotiations, as part of a total package offering them other satisfactions, that the developing countries can be expected to participate significantly in any agreemen' on TRIMS.

Trade in Services

The negotiations on services have been formally assigned to a separate Negotiating Group, working parallel with the Group of Negotiations on Goods, but reporting to the Trade Negotiations Committee.

The Uruguay Declaration defined the objective of these negotiations as being:

> to establish a multilateral framework of principles and rules for trade in services, including elaboration of possible disciplines for individual sectors, with a view to expansion of such trade under conditions of transparency and progressive liberalisation and as means of promoting economic growth of all trading partners and the development of developing countries. Such a framework shall respect the policy objectives of national laws and regulations applying to services and shall take into account the work of relevant international organisations.

While this formulation brings services into the ambit of the multilateral negotiations of the Uruguay Round, it clearly reflects the cautiousness of the approach and the real difficulties to be expected in the course of the negotiations. In particular, perhaps, it reflects the potential conflict between progress in liberalisation by the opening up of access to markets on GATT principles of open trade and existing systems of both national and international regulation.

The early discussions in the Group of Negotiations on Services served to emphasise these aspects. The group defined the elements to be addressed as part of its work programme. These were set out as being:

- Definitional and statistical issues
- Broad concepts on which principles and rules for trade in services, including possible disciplines for individual sectors, might be based
- Coverage of the multilateral framework for trade in services
- Existing international disciplines and arrangements
- Measures and practices contributing to or limiting the expansion of trade in services, including specifically any barriers perceived by individual participants, to which the conditions of transparency and progressive liberalisation might be applicable.

It was envisaged that work on these lines would occupy at least the whole of 1987, and this proved to be the case.

Throughout the year, the discussions in the Negotiating Group saw the lines drawn between the United States, Japan and Canada on the one side, and India and Brazil, supported by many of the developing-country participants, on the other. The United States continued to press for an early start to negotiations about principles and the construction of a framework agreement which could begin to apply to individual sectors during 1988. It did little, however, in the early part of 1987, to move the debate from broad generalities to the practicalities of negotiating any sort of a text. Canada made rather more specific suggestions about rules on the transparency of regulatory systems, and about compiling an inventory of "perceived" barriers as a basic starting point for negotiation, But it was clear from the nature of the U.S. interventions that a lot of hard work would be needed before even the shape, let alone a text, of any set of rules could emerge.

Meanwhile, on the other side, India and Brazil continued to emphasise their view that the case for international rules—in particular, rules within the GATT, or based on the principles of the GATT—had not been fully established. They maintained that the first task was to do much more work on the definitional and statistical aspects, to look much more closely at the implications of liberalisation for the development prospects of developing countries and, in general, to debate much more thoroughly the five elements enunciated by the group—which became elevated to an almost sacrosanct status—before there could be any question of negotiation. In particular, they put great stress on the Declaration's reference to "respect" for "the policy objectives of national laws and regulations".

The European Community gave general support to the United States' view of the importance of making progress on negotiations about a framework, although without any specific commitment to the idea of trying to achieve some degree of implementation during 1988. The Community did try, however, to put some flesh on the concepts, but still in vague and general language. It refined its own objective—and what it saw as the desirable objective for the negotiations—in pragmatic, rather than in doctrinal terms, as being "the liberalisation of world markets for the widest possible range of internationally tradeable services, in particular through the elimination of protectionist obstacles". Neither the United States nor the European Community, however, gave any realistic indication of how a practical negotiating process could get itself beyond this level of generalisation and come to grips with actually reducing existing barriers. In the case of goods, this was achieved by the comparatively straightforward proposition that the only acceptable form of protection for domestic products was the customs tariff, that all other barriers to trade such as quantitative restrictions at the frontier or discriminatory internal regulations or changes inside the frontier, were categorically forbidden, subject only to exceptional provisions for such reasons as security, and must be dismantled, and that the tariff itself should be subject to progressive negotiations for mutual reductions. (Nor should it be overlooked that 40 years and seven Rounds of negotiations later, the process is far from completed.) No such comprehensive and far-reaching solution has emerged for services.

At the end of 1987, however, both the United States and the European Community made more detailed formal submissions to the group, which may have opened up fresh lines of debate in a more constructive way; and during the 1988 meetings, they followed up with further suggestions on possible ways to organize negotiations.

In its revised proposals, the United States makes no fundamental change in the views it has espressed consistently throughout. It does, however, spell out a good deal more specifically what it sees as the content of the general concepts: transparency, nondiscrimination (the obligation on which would apply only to signatories), national treatment, discipline on state-sanctioned monoplies and some ancillary measures. It defines the overall objective in much the same way as the Community did. It recognises the "sovereign right of every country to regulate its service industries", but it also stresses that the framework should deal with (but only with) "those measures whose purpose or effect is to restrict the access and operations of foreign service providers", and that the framework "must ensure against the adoption or application of measures whose purpose or effect is restrictive or distortive of trade". The United States sees the framework as applying to "cross border movement of services as well as to the establishment of foreign branches and subsidiaries for purposes of producing or delivering the service within the host country". The framework should also be "broad but flexible"; once its content has been agreed, it should be used as a point of reference for negotiating individual sector agreements "as needed". These would provide additional more detailed rules, and should allow for greater precision and flexibility in attaining appropriate degrees of liberalisation, depending on the sector in question. Finally, the U.S. proposals make no concession to "special and differential" treatment for developing countries; the United States sees the framework as "of benefit to every country, regardless of its stage of economic development". By "its progressive and time phased liberalization", the framework should "contribute to development in a positive way, without compromising any individual country's development objectives", and will enable "local consumers to utilize services bearing the most advanced technology with the lowest possible prices".

The European Community's submission, unlike that of the United States, eschews virtually entirely any discussion of the philosophy or content of the general concepts of nondiscrimination and national treatment, although it tries to clarify what transparency should mean. By implication, it takes nondiscrimination and national treatment for granted as elements of the system, and as embodied in a framework, although treating them rather as end products of the negotiating process. Describing the submission as a starting point only, the Community concentrates on the mechanics of the negotiating process. It defines the central issue as being "how to achieve a major expansion of trade in services, thereby boosting growth in the world economy, while respecting the policy objectives which have led to the international and national regulation of services and promoting the development of developing countries." To this end, it introduces a number of new ideas into the debate. First, is adds "sectoral appropriateness" to the list of concepts to be considered. This means the relevance and validitity of the other general concept, and the extent to which all or any of them might need to be examined and modified in relation to each sector, or to "activities within sectors." Progressive liberalisation of market access thus would rest on respect for policy objectives and the "appropriateness" of the regulations in each sector. This would require a process of examination of regulations. For this purpose, the Community proposes the establishment of a permanent Regulations Committee. This would have the task of "distinguishing regulations regarded as appropriate, and on which no further action should be taken pursuant to the agreement, from those regarded as inappropriate and hence subject to eventual elimination or amendment . . . . Appropriate rules would have to be developed to define the role of the Regulations Committee and to ensure practicable procedures."

The Community's submission goes into some detail about criteria for appropriateness, which correspond fairly well with the general principles enunciated by the United States. The two approaches are, however, quite different even though they both accept many of the same premises. The U.S. approach is *a priori,* general and ambitious; the European is more concerned with practical procedure, readier to compromise with existing practices and low key. Perhaps even more important in relation to the immediate future of the negotiations, the U.S. proposals seem to aim primarily at trying to secure early agreement on a broad general package, even if this means that there would be a comparatively small number of signatories (and very few of these developing countries), while the European Community seems to contemplate a much longer and more empirically based process which makes substantial gestures to the concerns of the developing countries, in the hope that the eventual outcome, over time, would bring in a much wider spread of signatories.

The U.S. and European submissions certainly have not converted India and Brazil, or many other developing countries, into enthusiasts for an agreement, based on GATT principles, on trade in services. But they have considerably illuminated and opened up the discussion. There is perhaps some feeling among the negotiators that there is now on the table a core of ideas which can be worked on, and that, despite all the difficulties, some framework agreement on services could be the end result. This will certainly not be achieved, however, simply by amending parts of the text of the GATT. Rather, it is much more likely to be either a separate "general agreement on services", or—perhaps more likely in the first place—a more modest agreed statement of aspirations and intentions. It is doubtful, however, whether anything approaching the U.S. objective can be achieved in the short term, even in this modest form.

Dispute Settlement and the Functioning of the GATT system

The GATT procedures and results on dispute settlement have always been a source of dissatisfaction for a number of countries. These countries have felt that the procedures tended to favour the larger and more powerful over the smaller, either because dispute settlement panels were reluctant to produce reports which might offend powerful countries or because, even when there have been clear panel findings of the contravention of rules, there is no effective enforcement machinery. Offending countries, especially the large ones, can either block GATT Council decisions condemning them—since the GATT's consensus traditions require their own acquiescence—or can simply disregard recommendations, since they do not face effective retaliatory action from injured parties.

Although such cases are the exception rather than the rule, and although there is general acceptance that the dispute procedures work well in most cases, there was enough disquiet on the subject for the Uruguay Declaration to include "dispute settlement" as one of the items for negotiation. The Declaration said that these negotiations should "aim to improve and strengthen the rules and procedures of the dispute settlement process, while recognising the contribution that would be made by more effective and enforceable GATT rules and disciplines".

On this basis, a separate Negotiating Group was set up. The discussions in the group seem to suggest a fair degree of convergence of views, especially on enhancement of conciliation and mediation processes, with recognition of the possibility of a more active—though probably not more public—role for the GATT Secretariat, improvements in specific procedures, including the setting of time limits, and the desirability of more effective methods of securing compliance with the implementation of Council recommendations.

But there is a difference of view and of emphasis between those who want to see a more juridical enforcement role for the GATT—the leading countries on this side are the United States and Canada—and those who put more stress on compromise and conciliation—the European Community and Brazil are the leaders of this view. A number of countries, again including Canada, have suggested that there should be a special form of Council procedure—which they call the Council's sitting "in dispute settlement mode"—in which the parties to a dispute might participate in discussions but would not take part in any deciding vote. This has been called the "consensus minus two" procedure. The European Community is the most outspoken critic of this suggestion, insisting on the importance of preserving consensus of the whole. The Japanese have also opposed it.

Dispute settlement procedures are clearly a different sort of negotiating topic, from, say, tariffs or rules about subsidies. There seems no reason why conclusions in this area should need to be regarded as part of the balance of an overall package at the end of the negotiations. It may well be possible, therefore, for enough convergence of view to emerge for some agreement to be reached and implemented before the end of the Uruguay Round—perhaps even by the time of the mid-term review (which is discussed in the next section).

One can make the same comment in regard to what the Uruguay Round has discussed under the heading "Functioning of the GATT System". On this, the Declaration said:

negotiations shall aim to develop understandings and arrangements:

(i) to enhance the surveillance in the GATT to enable regular monitoring of trade policies and practices of contracting parties and their impact on the functioning of the multilateral trading system;

(ii) to improve the overall effectiveness and decision-making of the GATT as an institution, including, *inter-alia,* through involvement of Ministers;

(iii) to increase the contribution of the GATT to achieving greater coherence in global economic policy-making through strengthening its relationship with other international organisations responsible for monetary and financial matters.

The discussions in the Negotiating Group seem to have followed this remit very closely, and without any marked dissension between either the United States and the European Community or other industralised countries, or between developed and developing countries. There have, of course, been differences of detail about the exact form of, for example, the involvement of Ministers or the shape of a system of review—the term now strongly preferred to "surveillance"—of trade policies. But it is reasonably likely that a consensus will emerge, as a result of which regular periodic reviews of the trade policies of Contracting Parties will take place and will be published—perhaps strengthening public awareness of the importance of international trade policy; ministers will be involved more regularly and more directly in the working of the GATT as an institution—thereby strengthening the political will of governments in the liberal trade process; and there should be stronger links among the international economic institutions. Much of this echoes, at last, the recommendations of the Leutwiler Report and those made by the International Chamber of Commerce as long ago as 1983. However, the Negotiating Group has not, apparently, gone so far as to accept what those recommendations saw as an important element in securing public attention: the establishment of a strong and independent Permanent Survey Body, designed to enhance the authority and prestige of reports prepared by a much-strengthened GATT Secretariat.

The European Community has now formally put forward proposals on the lines of the consensus emerging in the Negotiating Group. The Community spells out the idea of enhancing GATT's status and political clout. It proposes that, within the GATT and supported by increased resources available to the Secretariat, a trade policy review mechanism be created which would produce regular country reports. These would be examined at special sessions of the GATT Council, and published with the Council's comments. They would not be perceived as judgement on countries' policies but as providing public and authoritative information. They would also promote the role of the GATT in the process of global economic policymaking. The United States, Japan and other countries already have backed much of this, so there seems a fair chance of progress in this area in advance of the completion of the Uruguay Round.

CHAPTER X

"Early Harvest" and the Mid-Term Review

The ink was barely dry on the text of the Uruguay Declaration when the United States began to campaign for an "early harvest" of "concrete results" for at least some of the elements among the matters to be taken up in the negotiations. Nor were the announced aims about what might be secured in this early harvest at all modest. Agriculture, services, trade-related intellectual property measures, even trade-related investment measures—which, for most participating countries at that stage, was little more than a half-understood phase—were all mentioned as areas on which it was important, indeed essential, to make quick progress.

The United States' motivation in this was, of course, easy to understand. The Administration, wrestling with a surge of protectionism in Congress and its manifestations in the texts of legislation then under way in both the House of Representatives and the Senate, felt that it must demonstrate its zeal in the task of persuading the United States' trading partners to help in damping down the worst of the protectionist excesses. One may well argue that to excite congressional hopes of an early outcome on these lines, and to envisage as possibilities prospects which on any sober calculation were utopian, might well have turned out to be counterproductive. One can, on the other hand, argue that in pitching claims and objectives at a much higher than realistic level, the United States eventually might achieve more than by pursuing more modest and pedestrian tactics.

Whether as a result of the continuing U.S. pressure, or only partly on that account and partly because it is a sensible thing to do, the participants in the Uruguay Round have agreed on a mid-term review of progress in the Round so far. This will take place in Montreal in December 1988, and will be undertaken by a meeting of the Trade Negotiations Committee at the Ministerial Level—that is, by a meeting of Trade Ministers.

In references to this meeting, the formal documents avoid the use of language which suggests that Montreal will be the occasion for concluding any agreements on any of the topics under negotiation, in advance of the ending of the Round. It is, of course, part of the doctrine of the GATT Rounds that the final outcome is a balanced package, in which each of the participants can feel that the totality of the bargain—the pluses and minuses of benefits and concessions—is advantageous. Everyone must win, and everyone must have prizes; this, indeed, is not an unfair judgement. The Montreal meeting, therefore, could be simply a review of the progress made so far over all the topics under negotiation, with the implied suggestion that by the injection of the political factor at this comparatively early stage—much earlier than in previous operations—some additional boost will be given to the process. Similarily, the Ministerial review could serve to bring to light elements of special political difficulty for particular participants, and thus secure greater understanding of the problems by the other participants.

It is fairly clear that, generally speaking, this is the role for the mid-term review that the European Community and—except on one or two topics of special interest to them—most of the developing countries would find most acceptable. For a few more "achievist" countries, however, this quiet approach would be, or would be described as, a great disappointment. The leaders on this side are the United States, Canada, Australia and, to a limited extent, Japan. The Australians—most ambitiously of all—have listed agriculture, dispute settlement, tropical products, "some progress" on safeguards, a framework agreement on services, something on the functioning of the GATT and a clear indication of how to move forward on tariffs and on market access generally, as their desiderata. The United States has advanced a more modest list, but still presents itself as clinging to the hope that agriculture and services would have substantive progress to show. Many developing countries would like to see some agreement on tropical products, as well as an indication that the major developed countries will be ready to show their willingness to bring the Multifibres Arrangement to an end when its present term runs out in 1991. All of them—and some developed countries, too—hope that there is better evidence of observance of the standstill and rollback commitments by the time of the Montreal meeting.

Looking at the situation realistically, in mid-1988, it seems inescapable to take any other view than that, over much the greater part of the field, Montreal can be little more than a stock-taking exercise, with some hope of a few prods for some items, but also with recognition of inevitably slow progress on others. On agriculture, especially, the persistent difference in approach between the European Community and the United States, and the internal policy stresses of the Community, are not conducive to an early advance toward general liberalisation. The most that seems capable of achievement might be agreement on, and perhaps fairly early implementation of, some emergency, short-term measures to alleviate problems of surplus supplies in a few of the most dangerous commodity areas. (The pressure for this kind of action however, has in any case been lessened by the effect of weather conditions during 1988.) On services, it stills seems likely that, in spite of some movement in the debate, the combination of the reluctance of the main developing countries and the sheer technical and intellectual complexity and elusiveness of the issues will severely limit the possibilities of substantial progress.

There are some areas, however, which might hold the promise of sufficient concrete achievement to give Montreal a measure of success in the way of agreements reached in advance of the conclusion of the Round. Tropical products, disputes settlement and improvements in the functioning of the GATT machinery—by, say, establishing the kind of survey process described above and investing it with some authority and resources—are matters which can reasonably be detatched from the bargaining process. This process dictates that virtually all the other topics—especially, at least in the European Community's view, agriculture—must be regarded as part of the total negotiating package, and cannot be dealt with at all easily in a substantive way until the content of the total package can be discerned.

The communiqué at the end of the Montreal meeting might, therefore, have to be content with emollient mid-term reporting, in guardedly optimistic terms, on the work of most of the Negotiating Groups. But if it can report agreement on tropical products, on dispute settlement machinery and on the establishment of a better, more efficient, and more publicly visible and authoritative institutional presence for the GATT, it will be able to claim a modest degree of success for the work of the first two years of the Uruguay Round.

CHAPTER XI

Conclusion

This survey of the events during the period from the November 1982 Ministerial Session of the GATT in Geneva, to the September 1986 Ministerial Meeting in Punte del Este which produced the Uruguay Declaration, of the subsequent progress of negotiations in Geneva and of the main topics under discussion up to mid-1988 has deliberately left out or mentioned only in passing a number of major elements in the world trade policy environment. These factors were just beginning to be significant as the Punta del Este meeting approached, or have developed much more significantly during the months since the Declaration was announced. It seemed best to organize the material in this way partly to preserve the continuity and unity of the narrative and partly because these matters, although they are of fundamental importance for the further progress of the Uruguay Round and its ultimate conclusions, have not had much direct or decisive effect on the negotiations so far. There was bound to be an initial period of procedural manouvering and of definitional, statistical and fact-compiling exercises alongside the process of exploration and clarification of concepts and ideas before the real business of negotiations on substance got into its stride. This is, in fact, what has been happening in the period since September 1986. But now that substantive negotiations should be beginning in earnest, the matters to be discussed in the following paragraphs are bound to be of direct and basic relevance to future progress.

This concluding section, therefore, looks at the wider background matters. It then draws together the threads in a summary analysis of the central matters at issue, both in relation to the overall objectives of the Round and to the shorter-term outlook for the mid-term review in December 1988 in Montreal.

Far and away the most important of the background topics is the question of U.S. trade policy legislation, and the negotiating power available under it to the U.S. Administration and its negotiators, together with the U.S. elections in November 1988 and the end of the Reagan presidency in January 1989. The U.S. constitution gives to Congress, not to the president or his representatives, control over international trade policy, and it is only under authority granted to the president by legislation that the U.S. negotiators can arrive at agreements with other countries. This does not mean that the Administration cannot negotiate, but it does mean that it cannot, except within the limits of authority delegated to it, arrive at binding conclusions.

Throughout the period of the Uruguay Round negotiations so far,—just as in the early period of the Tokyo Round—new trade policy legislation has been under consideration in Congress. The legislation deals with many aspects of U.S. trade policy in general as well as with the definition of the scope of, and limits on, the president's authority. It has also become immensely complicated by accretions dealing with many aspects of international economic policy besides trade, and with a number of matters of internal industrial and economic policy. The shape of the strictly international trade aspects of the legislation— somewhat different versions were making their respective ways through the Senate and the House of Representatives—has been much influenced by the substantial growth of protectionist pressures in the United States over recent years.

At one time, it seemed quite possible that the elaborateness of the drafts being considered might mean that no legislation at all would emerge before the presidential election in November 1988, and that the whole process would have to begin again under a new president and with a new Congress in 1989. At best, there would have to be a mammoth process to reconcile the different versions from the two parts of Congress into a single bill for presentation to president. Even then, there was clearly a strong likelihood that the bill would be unacceptable to the Administration, and that the president would veto it. It was possible, therefore, that the current presidency and Congress would expire without trade legislation in place. On the other hand, there was also the clear possibility that the outcome would be legislation from which the worst protectionist excesses had been removed, and which the president would not feel able to veto, but would still contain many trade policy provisions which were repugnant to other countries and that would impose mandatory requirements on the president which would seriously threaten the Uruguay Round negotiating process. All these uncertainties were compounded by the fact that, in any case, there will be a new president and Congress in 1989, and that no certain predictions could be made about what sort of trade policy will be followed. This last uncertainty of course, will only be resolved following the election and development of U.S. policy thereafter.

In circumstances like these, other countries' negotiators are in a difficult position. Can they really make concessions on their own desiderata in return for concessions which the U.S. negotiators in the end may not be able to deliver? Can they even commit themselves firmly to particular courses without knowing the one on which the United States—still, after all, the most important world commercial power—is set? So long as these uncertainties exist, they are bound to contribute to an atmosphere which imposes on the Geneva negotiations some flavour of shadow boxing.

In the event, in May 1988, Congress did succeed in presenting an agreed bill to the president. It did, indeed contain some protectionist trade policy features which both the U.S. Administration and the rest of the world much disliked; and the president vetoed it. His veto, however, was *not* based on objections to the trade policy sections. After Congress reconsidered it and eliminated the provisions which had evoked the veto, it was accepted by the President, and has become the basis of U.S. trade policy and of the Administration's negotiating powers during the Uruguay Round.

The Act is much too complex to try to analyse here (see Appendix 9 for a summary of its provisions). It is, indeed, much more informed by economic nationalism and protectionist sentiment than any U.S. trade legislation since the 1930s. It is bound to affect many of the mechanisms of the implementation of U.S. trade law and policy in ways which may well exacerbate international conflicts and ill feeling in the years ahead. It probably gives the president and his negotiators adequate room for manoeuvre in the Uruguay Round, however, and unless the new Administration, from 1989 onward, shows itself to be radically changing the course and the direction of U.S. policy, it need not inhibit the negotiating process. Nonetheless, the sharper and less internationally minded atmosphere which this bill must impose on the U.S. negotiators—at any rate, in the perceptions of the rest of the world—cannot but be a negative rather than a positive influence on the negotiations as a whole. Moreover, in the hands of an Administration with less liberal views on trade policy, it could indeed be used for restrictive and protectionist purposes. It has already evoked criticism on these lines from the European Community, Japan, and others.

Closely allied to the question of the U.S. international trade legislation is the matter of the Canada-U.S. Free Trade Agreement, negotiations on which were brought to a close at the end of 1987. This has been finally approved in the United States. In Canada, however, there will be a General Election in which this issue is a central one, before the matter is settled. (A synopsis of the main elements of the Agreement is in Appendix 10.) The relationship between the United States and Canada is clearly unique. The fact of this Agreement—assuming it secures approval in both countries—is, however, of some significance for the Uruguay Round negotiations. On the one hand, the content of the Agreement throws light on U.S. attitudes toward some of the issues in the Round—the treatment of services and of investment measures, for example. (These are substantially in line with what has been said above in discussion of these issues.) On the other hand, the willingness of the United States to conclude bilateral free trade area agreements and the negotiating power it can command in doing so may indicate that this is an alternative route for U.S. international trade policy should there be a serious breakdown in Geneva. Nothing of that kind is openly on the table, but it cannot be ignored altogether in considering the overall picture. Remarks made by leading members of the U.S. Administration about the possibility of "free trade area" discussions with Japan further fuel speculation in this direction.

The third major matter to be considered is the general question of the relationships among the major participants in the Round: the United States, the European Community and Japan. This has been discussed in some detail in describing events leading up to Punte del Este, but one must also look at developments since. There has been less open attack on each others' policies recently than was in the air during most of 1986 and the earlier part of 1987. But the roots of conflict have not died, and are liable to resurface at any time. The number of items at issue between the United States and the European Community continues to increase. By far the majority, but by no means all, of these are related to the treatment of agricultural commodities. The United States still bitterly attacks the Community's subsidies, particularly those to oilseed producers. The Community retaliates by making complaints against long-term U.S. restrictions on imports of sugar, dairy produce, cotton and groundnuts. One particularly difficult cause of contention affects the whole tripartite relationship. This is an agreement between the United States and Japan which not only limited imports of Japanese semiconductors into the United States, but also aimed to impose some measure of control on the prices charged for Japanese exports of semiconductors elsewhere in the world — including to the European Community — in order to limit their competitive effect on U.S. exports. The situation was further exacerbated when the United States imposed punitive tariffs on a substantial volume of imports from Japan in retaliation for what it regarded as inadequate implementation of the agreement. Meanwhile, the European Community has assailed the agreement itself as a contravention of the GATT. It saw tariffs, therefore, as an illegal attempt to enforce an illegal agreement, and a GATT panel has declared at least some aspects of the agreement to be in contravention of the GATT.

Concomitantly, there has also been a sharpening of conflict between the European Community and Japan, partly in consequence of U.S. actions, and partly from continuing and apparently endemic anti-Japanese action and sentiment in the Community. There have been intensified anti dumping procedures, directed against components imported for local assembly, threats of trade retaliation in response to perceived Japanese denial of access for financial and other services and periodically renewed emphasis on bilateral imbalances.

Finally, there seems to be some increasing unease in countries outside the European Community about the possible effects of the much closer ties of economic integration inside the Community to be created by the completion of the internal Community market by 1992.

The objective of the 1992 programme, embodied in the Single European Act enacted by the legislatures of all 12 members of the Community, is to establish by that date a truly unified, single market without internal frontiers. There has been no suggestion from leaders of the Community countries that this reinforcement of their unity—to whatever extent it may in the event be achieved by 1992 or within measurable distance of that date—is intended to create, alongside the removal of internal barriers, any intensification of external ones. But there is no doubt that the rest of the world is feeling at worst considerable apprehension and at best a great deal of anxious uncertainty about what the effects of "1992" might be for their trade and economic relations with this looming economic superpower.

All these events must certainly be regarded as dangerous time bombs ticking somewhat ominously not so very far below the surface. Meanwhile, however, it is a relief to recognise that the negotiating process in Geneva is still reasonably on course. On that basis, one can sum up the outlook and prospects on the central issues on the following lines:

1. *Standstill and rollback*

   The performance of the major trading countries on their commitment to standstill and rollback continues to be unsatisfactory to the developing countries, and is likely to come under much criticism at the mid-term review. In the long term, it will be difficult to claim "success" for the Uruguay Round without some progress on this issue, since it is precisely conduct of the kind covered by these commitments that the Round is designed to remedy.

2. *Tariffs*

   There will, no doubt, be a tariff agreement at the end of the Round, but the tariff negotiations are not by any means the most important element.

3. *Agriculture*

   It is still difficult to see a result on agriculture, certainly in the short term, and even in the final outcome, which will measure up to the high aspirations of restoring the disciplines of the international trading system. This will be greatly disappointing to the agricultural countries that have joined together in the Cairns Group. It might be possible to achieve some short-term emergency measures. In the long term, however, domestic pressures seem the more likely engine to bring about a thoroughgoing reform of agricultural policies, when the non-agricultural sections of the population eventually realise the cost that existing policies impose on them, on their national economies and on the world as a whole. The international negotiations, however, can be a valuable additional means of pressure.

4. *Safeguards*

The debate on safeguards seems to remain as intractable as it has been since it began in earnest in the 1970s. It seems unlikely that the mid-term review will be able to do more than report, in suitably emollient language, what discussion has taken place. The final issues will remain whether, and if so under what conditions, emergency safeguard action against imports can be undertaken "selectively" rather than on a nondiscriminatory basis, and how to deal with the grey-area measures which have proliferated. If the Uruguay Round negotiators suceed in finding an acceptable solution to those issues, that in itself will justify the Round.

5. *Trade related aspects of intellectual property rights (TRIPS) and of investment measures (TRIMS)*

These are both topics on which a good deal of exploratory work has still to be done—much more, of course, on TRIMS than on TRIPS. On balance, there seems a fair chance that, at the end of the day, considerable progress may be made on TRIPS, but it does not seem feasible to see a completed agreement in time for the mid-term review. TRIMS is a more elusive and difficult topic, but the Round at least will have put the more apparent trade-related aspects—performance requirements and local content rules—on to the international agenda, and may achieve some progress toward international understanding.

6. *Services*

It is a matter of the highest importance for world prosperity that some significant advance be made toward a system of international rules for trade in services during the Uruguay Round. In one way or another, this probably will be achieved. There are still differences of approach between the major industrialised countries and the leading developing countries, and some differences of emphasis, and of attitudes on negotiating technique, among the United States, Japan, Canada and the European Community. There must be some doubt about how substantial a framework can be put into shape in any short term. It would be a real failure of international leadership, however, if there were not some significant advance by the end of the Round.

The Mid-Term Review and After

The Montreal meeting of Trade Ministers of countries participating in the Round at the end of 1988 will have before it a substantial volume of documentation, including the progress reports from each of the 14 Negotiating Groups, the Group of Negotiations on Goods, the Group of Negotiations on Services and the Standstill and Rollback Surveillance Body. Presumably, all these will be brought together as a comprehensive Report to the Trade Negotiations Committee, the overseeing authority in the negotiations.

Over a large part of this complex of topics, it seems unlikely that the Ministers will be able to do more than to take note of progress so far and, perhaps, to provide some agreed guidance at the political level, which might assuage some of the negotiating frictions. But more concrete results of a substantive kind on at least some topics will be needed if the mid-term review is not to be written off as a setback to the Round rather than a stimulus to its future progress. The most likely candidates for such results will be in those areas which may be regarded as capable of being considered on their own merits as separate from the "package" of benefits and concessions which each participant will have to assess at the end of the whole process. The most obvious topic of this kind are the important, but procedural rather than operational, ones of dispute settlement and the functioning of the GATT system. These are not really matters for the give and take of bargaining. There does seem to be a fair chance that useful changes can be agreed during 1988. On dispute settlement, there could be largely technical improvements, including the introduction of firm deadlines for the various satges of the operation, and some better procedure for ensuring the implementation of agreed findings. On the mechanics and working of the system, there might emerge a strengthened and more publicly influential system of regular review of trade policy actions of all Contracting Parties. More regular involvement of Ministers in GATT processes, designed to increase the political impact and efficient operation of international disciplines, is also possible.

There also seems to be a fair chance that the mid-term review may show results in agreement on the treatment by the developed countries of imports of tropical products. This, if it can be achieved, would be a sort of advance concession to the developing countries, and would no doubt improve the negotiating atmosphere on a number of other topics, where conflict between developed and developing countries is sometimes even more stultifying to progress than the differences of view between the United States and the European Community. Such outcome, especially if it is accompanied by the prospect of improved performance on the standstill and rollback commitments, could be regarded as a reasonably satisfactory result of the first two years of the Round. It would fall short of the much-publicized aspirations of the U.S. Administration, and of the professed hopes of some other countries, but it cannot be much less than they could realistically expect.

What happens at the mid-term review will profoundly affect the course of negotiations thereafter, and the eventual outcome certainly will have to be reassessed in the light of that review. It is idle, therefore, to look further forward at this stage in any categorical way, although some tentative judgments were made earlier in this survey. To bring this study to a close, therefore, it may be appropriate to recall the final sentences of *The GATT Negotiations, 1973-75: A Guide to the Issues*, which was published in 1974 and which dealt with the Tokyo Round:

> In the present state of the world, and of international economic and political relations, it would be unrealistic and utopian to suppose that the GATT negotiations will, in short term, have very much more than marginal effects on either the scale and pattern of world trade or on the conduct of national policies. But it would be surely a too great counsel of despair to believe that the great trading powers of the world will not find, through these negotiations, the way to preserve and to restore the will and the means for continuing international cooperation and progress.

In 1988, one might have a rather less sceptical aspiration than the first of these two sentences expresses about the eventual effects of a successful outcome for the Uruguay Round. National policies, in some areas at any rate, are desperately in need of more than marginal change. And the second sentence now must be addressed not only to the "great trading powers", but also to the many other smaller countries that, to the world's great benefit, have established themselves successfully as important partners in international trade and in the decisions about its future which the remaining negotiations of the Uruguay Round will make.

Appendices

MINISTERIAL DECLARATION ON THE URUGUAY ROUND

Ministers, meeting on the occasion of the Special Session of CONTRACTING PARTIES at Punta del Este, have decided to launch Multilateral Trade Negotiatins (The Uruguay Round). To this end, they have adopted the following Declaration. The multilateral trade negotiations (MTN) will be open to the participation of countries as indicated in Parts I and II of this Declaration. A Trade Negotiations Committee (TNC) is established to carry out the negotiations. The Trade Negotiations Committee shall hold its first meeting not later than 31 October 1986. It shall meet as appropriate at Ministerial level. The Multilateral Trade Negotiations will be concluded within four years.

PART 1

NEGOTIATIONS ON TRADE IN GOODS

The CONTRACTING PARTIES meeting at Ministerial level

DETERMINED to halt and reverse protectionism and to remove distortions to trade

DETERMINED also to preserve the basic principles and to further the objectives of the GATT

DETERMINED also to develop a more open, viable and durable multilateral trading system

CONVINCED that such action would promote growth and development

MINDFUL of the negative effects of prolonged financial and monetary instability in the world economy, the indebtedness of a large number of less-developed contracting parties, and considering the linkage between trade, money, finance and development

DECIDE to enter into Multilateral Trade Negotiations on trade in goods within the framework and under the aegis of the General Agreement on Tariffs and Trade.

A. OBJECTIVES

Negotiations shall aim to:

(i) bring about further liberalization and expansion of world trade to the benefit of all countries, especially less-developed contracting parties, including the improvement of access to markets by the reduction and elimination of tariffs, quantitative restrictions and other non-tariff measures and obstacles;

(ii) strengthen the rôle of GATT, improve the multilateral trading system based on the principles and rules of the GATT and bring about a wider coverage of world trade under agreed, effective and enforceable multilateral disciplines;

(iii) increase the responsiveness of the GATT system to the evolving international economic environment, through facilitating necessary structural adjustment, enhancing the relationship of the GATT with the relevant international organizations and taking account of changes in trade patterns and prospects, including the growing importance of trade in high-technology products, serious difficulties in commodity markets and the importance of an improved trading environment providing, *inter alia*, for the ability of indebted countries to meet their financial obligations;

(iv) foster concurrent co-operative action at the national and international levels to strengthen the interrelationship between trade policies and other economic policies affecting growth and development, and to contribute towards continued, effective ad determined efforts to improve the functioning of the international monetary system and the flow of financial and real investment resources to developing countries.

B. GENERAL PRINCIPLES GOVERNING NEGOTIATIONS

(i) Negotiations shall be conducted in a transparent manner, and consistent with the objectives and commitments agreed in this Declaration and with the principles of the General Agreement in order to ensure mutual advantage and increased benefits to all participants.

(ii) The launching, the conduct and the implementation of the outcome of the negotiations shall be treated as parts of a single undertaking. However, agreements reached at an early stage may be implemented on a provisional or a definitive basis by agreement prior to the formal conclusion of the negotiations. Early agreements shall be taken into account in assessing the overall balance of the negotiations.

(iii) Balanced concessions should be sought within broad trading areas and subjects to be negotiated in order to avoid unwarranted cross-sectoral demands.

(iv) CONTRACTING PARTIES agree that the principle of differential and more favourable treatment embodied in Part IV and other relevant provisions of the General Agreement and in the Decision of the CONTRACTING PARTIES of 28 November 1979 on Differential and More Favourable Treatment, Reciprocity and Fuller Participation of Developing Countries applies to the negotiations. In the implementation of standstill and rollback, particular care should be given to avoiding disruptive effects on the trade of less-developed contracting parties.

(v) The developed countries do not expect reciprocity for commitments made by them in trade negotiations to reduce or remove tariffs and other barriers to the trade of developing countries, ie the developed countries do not expect the developing countries, in the course of trade negotiations, to make contributions which are inconsistent with their individual development, financial and trade needs. Developed contracting parties shall therefore not seek, neither shall less-developed contracting parties be required to make, concessions that are inconsistent with the latter's development, financial and trade needs.

(vi) Less-developed contracting parties expect that their capacity to make contributions or negotiated concessions or take other mutually agreed action under the provisions and procedures of the General Agreement would improve with the progressive development of their economies and improvement in their trade situation and they would accordingly expect to participate more fully in the framework of rights and obligations under the General Agreement.

(vii) Special attention shall be given to the particular situation and problems of the least-developed countries and to the need to encourage positive measures to facilitate expansion of their trading opportunities. Expeditious implementation of the relevant provisions of the 1982 Ministerial Declaration concerning the least-developed countries shall also be given appropriate attention.

C. STANDSTILL AND ROLLBACK

Commencing immediately and continuing until the formal completion of the negotiations, each participant agrees to apply the following commitments:

Standstill

(i)   not to take any trade restrictive or distorting measure inconsistent with the provisions of the General Agreement or the Instruments negotiated within the framework of GATT or under its auspices;

(ii) not to take any trade restrictive or distorting measure in the legitimate exercise of its GATT rights, that would go beyond that which is necessary to remedy specific situations, as provided for in the General Agreement and the Instruments referred to in (i) above;

(iii) not to take any trade measures in such a manner as to improve its negotiating positions.

Rollback

(i)   that all trade restrictive or distorting measures inconsistent with the provisions of the General Agreement of Instruments negotiated within the framework of GATT or under its auspices, shall be phased out or brought into conformity within an agreed timeframe not later than by the date of the formal completion of the negotiations, taking into account multilateral agreements, undertakings and understandings, including strengthened rules and disciplines, reached in pursuance of the objectives of the negotiations;

(ii) there shall be progressive implementation of this commitment on an equitable basis in consultations among participants concerned, including all affected participants. This commitment shall take account of the concerns expressed by any participant about measures directly affecting its trade interests;

(iii) there shall be no GATT concessions requested for the elimination of these measures.

Surveillance of standstill and rollback

Each participant agrees that the implementation of these commitments on standstill and rollback shall be subject to multilateral surveillance so as to ensure that these commitments are being met. The Trade Negotiations Committee will decide on the appropriate mechanisms to carry out the surveillance, including periodic reviews and evaluations. Any participant may bring to the attention of the appropriate surveillance mechanism any actions or omissions it believes to be relevant to the fulfilment of these commitments. These notifications should be addressed to the GATT secretariat which may also provide further relevant information.

D. SUBJECTS FOR NEGOTIATIONS

Tariffs

Negotiations shall aim, by appropriate methods, to reduce or, as appropriate, eliminate tariffs including the reduction or elimination of high tariffs and tariff escalation. Emphasis shall be given to the expansion of the scope of tariff concessions among all participants.

Non-tariff measures

Negotiations shall aim to reduce or eliminate non-tariff measures, including quantitative restrictions, without prejudice to any action to be taken in fulfilment of the rollback commitments.

Tropical products

Negotiations shall aim at the fullest liberalization of trade in tropical products, including in their processed and semi-processed forms and shall cover both tariff and all non-tariff measures affecting trade in these products.

CONTRACTING PARTIES recognize the importance of trade in tropical products to a large number of less-developed contracting parties and agree that negotiations in this area shall receive special attention, including the timing of the negotiations and the implementation of the results as provided for in B(ii).

Natural resource-based products

Negotiations shall aim to achieve the fullest liberalization of trade in natural resource-based products, including in their processed and semi-processed forms. The negotiations shall aim to reduce or eliminate tariff and non-tariff measures, including tariff escalation.

Textiles and clothing

Negotiations in the area of textiles and clothing shall aim to formulate modalities that would permit the eventual integration of this sector into GATT on the basis of strengthened GATT rules and disciplines, thereby also contributing to the objective of further liberalization of trade.

Agriculture

CONTRACTING PARTIES agree that there is an urgent need to bring more discipline and predictability to world agricultural trade by correcting and preventing restrictions and distortions including those related to structural surpluses so as to reduce the uncertainty, imbalances and instability in world agricultural markets.

Negotiations shall aim to achieve greater liberalization of trade in agriculture and bring all measures affecting import access and export competition under strengthened and more operationally effective GATT rules and disciplines, taking into account the general principles governing the negotiations, by:

(i)   improving market access through, *inter alia*, the reduction of import barriers;

(ii)   improving the competitive environment by increasing discipline on the use of all direct and indirect subsidies and other measures affecting directly or indirectly agricultural trade, including the phased reduction of their negative effects and dealing with their causes;

(iii) minimizing the adverse effects that sanitary and phytosanitary regulations and barriers can have on trade in agriculture, taking into account the relevant international agreements.

In order to achieve the above objectives, the negotiating group having primary responsibility for all aspects of agriculture will use the Recommendations adopted by the CONTRACTING PARTIES at their Fortieth Session, which were developed in accordance with the GATT 1982 Ministerial Programme and take account of the approaches suggested in the work of the Committee on Trade in Agriculture without prejudice to other alternatives that might achieve the objectives of the negotiations.

GATT Articles

Participants shall review existing GATT Articles, provisions and disciplines as requested by interested contracting parties, and, as appropriate, undertake negotiations.

Safeguards

(i)   A comprehensive agreement on safeguards is of particular importance to the strengthening of the GATT system and to progress in the MTNs.

(ii)   The agreement on safeguards:

- shall be based on the basic principles of the General Agreement;

- shall contain, *inter alia*, the following elements: transparency, coverage, objective criteria for action including the concept of serious injury or threat thereof, temporary nature, degressivity and structural adjustment, compensation and retaliation, notifications, consultation, multilateral surveillance and dispute settlement; and

- shall clarify and reinforce the disciplines of the General Agreement and should apply to all contracting parties.

MTN Agreements and Arrangements

Negotiations shall aim to improve, clarify, or expand, as appropriate, agreements and arrangements negotiated in the Tokyo Round of Multilateral Negotiations.

Subsidies and countervailing measures

Negotiations on subsidies and countervailing measures shall be based on a review of Articles VI and XVI and the MTN agreement on subsidies and countervailing measures with the objective of improving GATT disciplines relating to all subsidies and countervailing measures that affect international trade. A negotiating group will be established to deal with these issues.

Dispute settlement

In order to ensure prompt and effective resolution of disputes to the benefit of all contracting parties, negotiations shall aim to improve and strengthen the rules and the procedures of the dispute settlement process, while recognizing the contribution that would be made by more effective and enforceable GATT rules and disciplines. Negotiations shall include the development of adequate arrangements for overseeing and monitoring of the procedures that would facilitate compliance with adopted recommendations.

Trade-related aspects of intellectual property rights, including trade in counterfeit goods

In order to reduce the distortions and impediments to international trade, and taking into account the need to promote effective and adequate protection of intellectual property rights, and to ensure that measures and procedures to enforce intellectual property rights do not themselves become barriers to legitimate trade, the negotiations shall aim to clarify GATT provisions and elaborate as appropriate new rules and disciplines.

Negotiations shall aim to develop a multilateral framework of principles, rules and disciplines dealing with international trade in counterfeit goods, taking into account work already undertaken in the GATT.

These negotiations shall be without prejudice to other complementary initiatives that may be taken in the World Intellectual Property Organization and elsewhere to deal with these matters.

Trade-related investment measures

Following an examination of the operation of GATT Articles related to the trade restrictive and distorting effects of investment measures, negotiations should elaborate, as appropriate, further provisions that may be necessary to avoid such adverse effects on trade.

E. FUNCTIONING OF THE GATT SYSTEM

Negotiations shall aim to develop understandings and arrangements:

(i) to enhance the surveillance in the GATT to enable regular monitoring of trade policies and practices of contracting parties and their impact on the functioning of the multilateral trading system;

(ii)   to improve the overall effectiveness and decision-making of the GATT as an institution, including, *inter alia,* through involvement of Ministers;

(iii)   to increase the contribution of the GATT to achieving greater coherence in global economic policy-making through strengthening its relationship with other international organizations responsible for monetary and financial matters.

F. PARTICIPATION

(a)   Negotiations will be open to:
(1) all contracting parties,

(2) countries having acceded provisionally,

(3) countries applying the GATT on a *de facto* basis having announced, not later than 30 April 1987, their intention to accede to the GATT and to participate in the negotiations,

(4) countries that have already informed the CONTRACTING PARTIES, at a regular meeting of the Council of Representatives, of their intention to negotiate the terms of their membership as a contracting party, and

(5) developing countries that have, by 30 April 1987, initiated procedures for accession to the GATT, with the intention of negotiating the terms of their accession during the course of the negotiations.

(b)   Participation in negotiations relating to the amendment or application of GATT provisions or the negotiation of new provisions will, however, be open only to contracting parties.

G. ORGANIZATION OF THE NEGOTIATIONS

A Group of Negotiations on Goods (GNG) is established to carry out the programme of negotiations contained in this Part of the Declaration. The GNG shall, *inter alia*;

(i)   elaborate and put into effect detailed trade negotiating plans prior to 19 December 1986;

(ii)   designate the appropriate mechanism for surveillance of commitments to standstill and rollback;

(iii)   establish negotiating groups as required. Because of the interrelationship of some issues and taking fully into account the general principles governing the negotiations as stated in B(iii) above it is recognized that aspects of one issue may be discussed in more than one negotiating group. Therefore each negotiating group should as required take into account relevant aspects emerging in other groups;

(iv)   also decide upon inclusion of additional subject matters in the negotiations;

(v)   co-ordinate the work of the negotiating groups and supervise the progress of the negotiations. As a guideline not more than two negotiating groups should meet at the same time;

(vi)   the GNG shall report to the Trade Negotiations Committee.

In order to ensure effective application of differential and more favourable treatment the GNG shall, before the formal completion of the negotiations, conduct an evaluation of the results attained therein in terms of the Objectives and the General Principles Governing Negotiations as set out in the Declaration, taking into account all issues of interest to less-developed contracting parties.

PART II

NEGOTIATIONS ON TRADE IN SERVICES

Ministers also decided, as part of the Multilateral Trade Negotiations, to launch negotiations on trade in services.

Negotiations in this area shall aim to establish a multilateral framework of principles and rules for trade in services, including elaboration of possible disciplines for individual sectors, with a view to expansion of such trade under conditions of transparency and progressive liberalization and as a means of promoting economic growth of all trading partners and the development of developing countries. Such framework shall respect the policy objectives of national laws and regulations applying to services and shall take into account the work of relevant international organizations.

GATT procedures and practices shall apply to these negotiations. A Group on Negotiations on Services is established to deal with these matters. Participation in the negotiations under this Part of the Declaration will be open to the same countries as under Part I. GATT secretariat support will be provided, with technical support from other organizations as decided by the Group on Negotiations on Services.

The Group on Negotiations on Services shall report to the Trade Negotiations Committee.

APPENDIX 2

GATT MEMBERSHIP

CONTRACTING PARTIES TO THE GATT (96)

Antigua and Barbuda	Germany, Fed. Rep.	Niger
Argentina	Chana	Nigeria
Australia	Greece	Norway
Austria	Guyana	Pakistan
Bangladesh	Haiti	Peru
Barbados	Hong Kong	Philippines
Belgium	Hungary	Poland
Belize	Iceland	Portugal
Benin	India	Romania
Botswana	Indonesia	Rwanda
Brazil	Ireland	Senegal
Burkina Faso	Israel	Sierra Leone
Burma	Italy	Singapore
Burundi	Jamaica	South Africa
Cameroon	Japan	Spain
Canada	Kenya	Sri Lanka
Central African Republic	Korea, Rep.	Suriname
Chad	Kuwait	Sweden
Chile	Lesotho	Switzerland
Colombia	Luxembourg	Tanzania
Congo	Madagascar	Thailand
Côte d'Ivoire	Malawi	Togo
Cuba	Malaysia	Trinidad and Tobago
Cyprus	Maldives	Turkey
Czechoslovakia	Malta	Uganda
Denmark	Mauritania	United Kingdom
Dominican Republic	Mauritius	United States of America
Egypt	Mexico	Uruguay
Finland	Morocco	Yugoslavia
France	Netherlands	Zaire
Gabon	New Zealand	Zambia
Gambia	Nicaragua	Zimbabwe

Acceded provisionally (1): Tunisia

Countries to whose territories the GATT has been applied and which now, as independent States, maintain a *de facto* application of the GATT pending final decisions as to their future commercial policy (28)

Algeria	Guinea-Bissau	St. Vincent
Angola	Kampuchea	Sao Tomé and Principe
Bahamas	Kiribati	Seychelles
Bahrain	Mali	Solomon Islands
Brunei Darussalam	Mozambique	Swaziland
Cape Verde	Papua New Guinea	Tonga
Dominica	Qatar	Tuvalu
Equatorial Guinea	St. Christopher and Nevis	United Arab Emirates
Fiji	St. Lucia	Yemen, Democratic
Grenada		

Source: GATT Information, Geneva, 1988.

APPENDIX 3

MTM AGREEMENTS – Legal Status as of 4 September 1987

COUNTRIES Contracting Parties		Geneva 1979 Protocol	Suppl 1979 Protocol	Tech. Barriers	Gov't Procur.	Subsid Counter-vail	Bovine Meat	Dairy	Customs Val.	Import Lic.	Civil Aircraft	Anti-Dumping
Antigua and Barbuda	AB											
Argentina	AR	A		S	O	O	A	A	A*	S	O	O
Australia	AD		A	S	O	O	A	A	A*	S	O	O
Austria	AT	A		A	A	A	A		A	A	A	A
Bangladesh	AD			O	O	O	O	O	O	O	O	O
Barbados	BB											
Belgium	BE	A	A	A							A	
Belize	BZ					Prov.						
Benin	BJ											
Botswana	BW							A*				
Brazil	BR	A	A	O	A	A	O		A*	O	O	A
Burkin'a Faso												
Burma	BU											
Burundi	BI											
Cameroon	CM			O					O		O	
Canada	CA	A	A	A	A	A	A	O	A*	A	A	A
Cent.Afr.Rep.	CF											
Chad	TD											
Chile	CL	A	A	O	A	O	O	O	O		A	O
Colombia	CO			O		O	A		O	O		O
Congo	CG											
Côte d'Ivoire	CI	A		O	O	O	O	O	O	O		O
Cuba	CU			O	O	O	O	O	O	O		O
Cyprus	CY											
Czechoslovakia	CS	A		A*	O	O			A	A	O	A
Denmark	DK	A*		A*							A*	
Dominican Rep	DO			A	O	O				O		
Egypt	EG	A		A	O	A	A	S	O	A	S	A
EEC	CE	A	A	A	A	A	A	A	A	A	A	A
Finland	FI	A		A	A	A	A	A	A	A		A
France	FR	A		A							A	
Gabon	GA			O	O	O	O	O	O	O		
Gambia	GM											
Germany	DE	A*		A*							A*	
Ghana	GH			O		O			O		O	O
Greece	GR			S							S	
Guyana	GY											
Haiti	HT			A				O				
Hong Kong	HK			A	A	A			A	A		A
Hungary	HU	A		A*	O	O	A	A	A	A		A
Iceland	IS	A										
India	IN	A		A	O	A	O	O	A*	A	O	A
Indonesia	ID			A	O	O	A*		O	O	O	O
Ireland	IE	A		A							A	
Israel	IL	S		A	O	A	A*	O	O	O	O	O
Italy	IT	A		A							A	
Jamaica	JM	A				O			O			O

COUNTRIES Contracting Parties		Geneva 1979 Protocol	Suppl 1979 Protocol	Tech. Barriers	Gov't Procur.	Subsid Counter-vail	Bovine Meat	Dairy	Customs Val.	Import Lic.	Civil Aircraft	Anti-Dumping
Japan	JP	A*		A	A	A	A	A	A	A	A	A
Kenya	KE				O		O					
Korea	KR		A	A	O	A			A*	O		A
Kuwait	KW											
Luxembourg	LU	A		A							A	
Madagascar	MG			O			O					
Malawi	MW								A*			
Malaysia	MY		A	O	O	O			O	O		O
Maldives	MV											
Malta	MT			O	O	O	O	O		O	O	O
Mauritania	MR											
Mauritius	MU											
Mexico	MX			S		O	O	O	S	S		S
Morocco	MO											
Netherlands	NL	A		A							A	
New Zealand	NZ	A		A	O	A	A	A	A*	A		O
Nicaragua	NI			O	O	O	O	O	O	O		O
Niger	NE											
Nigeria	NG			O	O	O	A	O	O	A	O	O
Norway	NO	A		A	A	A	A	A	A	A	A	A
Pakistan	PK		A	A		A			O	A		A
Peru	PE		A	O	O	O			O	O		O
Philippines	PE			A	O	A*			O	A*		O
Poland	PL	A		O		O	A	A	O	A	O	A
Portugal	PT			A							A	
Romania	RO	A		A	O	O	A	A	A	A	A	A
Rwanda	RW			S								
Senegal	SN			O		O				O		O
Sierra Leone	SL											
Singapore	SG		A	A	A	O			O	A	O	A
South Africa	SA	A			O	O	A	A	A	A		O
Spain	ES	A	A	A		A			A		A	A
Sri Lanka	LK			O		O			O	O		O
Suriname	SR											
Sweden	SE	A		A	A	A	A	A	A	A	A	A
Switzerland	CE	A		A	A	A	A	A	A	A	A	A
Tanzania	TZ			O		O				O		O
Thailand	TE			O	O	O	O			O	O	O
Togo	TO											
Trin & Tob.	TT			O	O	O	O	O	O	O	O	O
Turkey	TR			O	O	A	O	O	S	O	O	O
Uganda	UG											
United Kingdom	GB	A		A*	A*				A*	A*	A*	
United States	US	A		A	A	A	A		A	A	A	A
Uruguay	UY		A			A	A	A				O
Yugoslavia	YU	A		A		S	A	O	A	A	O	A
Zaire	ZR		A	O	O	O	O		O	O	O	O
Zambia	ZM											
Zimbabwe	ZW			O								

COUNTRIES Contracting Parties		Geneva 1979 Protocol	Suppl 1979 Protocol	Tech. Barriers	Gov't Procur.	Subsid Counter-vail	Bovine Meat	Dairy	Customs Val.	Import Lic.	Civil Aircraft	Anti-Dumping
Other Countries												
Bulgaria	BG			O		O	A	A	O	O		O
China	CH			O	O				O	O		
Costa Rica	CR						O					
Ecuador	EC			O	O	O			O	O		O
Guatemala	GT						A*					
Lesotho	LS								A*			
Panama	PA						O	O				
Paraguay	PY						Prov					
Tunisia**	TN			A		O	A	O		O	O	O
Venezuela	VE					O				O		

A: Accepted   S: Signed (acceptance pending)   O: Observer   *Reservation, condition and/or declaration

Source: GATT Geneva 1987

[1] English only
[2] Including Protocol. Upon entry into force of the Agreement on 1 January 1981, the provisions of the Protocol were deemed to be an integral part of the Agreement

** Provisional accession to GATT.

RECOMMENDATIONS OF THE LEUTWILER GROUP

1.   In each country, the making of trade policy should be brought into the open. The costs and benefits of trade policy actions, existing and prospective, should be analyzed through a "protection balance sheet". Private and public companies should be required to reveal in their financial statements any subsidies received. Public support for open trade policies should be fostered.

2.   Agricultural trade should be based on clearer and fairer rules, with no special treatment for particular countries or commodities. Efficient agricultural producers should be given the maximum opportunity to compete.

3.   A timetable and procedures should be established to bring into conformity with GATT rules voluntary export restraints, orderly marketing agreements, discriminatory import restrictions, and other trade policy measures of both developed and developing countries which are inconsistent with the obligations of contracting parties under the GATT.

4.   Trade in textiles and clothing should be fully subject to the ordinary rules of the GATT.

5.   Rules on subsidies need to be revised, clarified and made more effective. When subsidies are permitted they should be granted only after full and detailed scrutiny.

6.   The GATT "codes" governing non-tariff distortions of trade should be improved and vigorously applied to make trade more open and fair.

7.   The rules permitting customs unions and free-trade areas have been distorted and abused. To prevent further erosion of the multilateral trading system, they need to be clarified and tightened up.

8.   At the international level, trade policy and the functioning of the trading system should be made more open. Countries should be subject to regular oversight or surveillance of their policies and actions, about which the GATT Secretariat should collect and publish information.

9.   When emergency "safeguard" protection for particular industries is needed, it should be provided only in accordance with the rules: it should not discriminate between different suppliers, should be time-limited, should be linked to adjustment assistance, and should be subject to continuing surveillance.

10. Developing countries receive special treatment in the GATT rules. But such special treatment is of limited value. Far greater emphasis should be placed on permitting and encouraging developing countries to take advantage of their competitive strengths, and on integrating them more fully into the trading system, with all the appropriate rights and responsibilities that this entails.

11. Governments should be ready to examine ways and means of expanding trade in services, and to explore whether multilateral rules can appropriately be devised for this sector.

12. In support of improved and strengthened rules, GATT's dispute settlement procedures should be reinforced by building up a permanent roster of non-governmental experts to examine disputes, and by improving the implementation of panel recommendations. Third parties should use their rights to complain when bilateral agreements break the rules.

13. We support the launching of a new round of GATT negotiations, provided they are directed toward the primary goal of strengthening the multilateral trading system and further opening world markets.

14. To ensure continuous high-level attention to problems in international trade policy, and to encourage prompt negotiation of solutions to them, a permanent Ministerial-level body should be established in GATT.

15. The health and even the maintenance of the trading system, and the stability of the financial system, are linked to a satisfactory resolution of the world debt problem, adequate flows of development finance, better international co-ordination of macro-economic policies, and greater consistency between trade and financial policies.

APPENDIX 5

MINISTERIAL MEETING OF FAIR TRADERS IN AGRICULTURE CAIRNS, AUSTRALIA, AUGUST 1986

BACKGROUND

Ministers and representatives of key fair trading countries in agriculture met in Cairns, Australia, 25-27 August 1986, to consider the crisis in world agricultural trade and to identify areas of co-operation and common strategies to bring about lasting solutions.

Ministers, senior officials and farm industry leaders from Argentina, Australia, Brazil, Canada, Chile, Colombia, Fiji, Hungary, Indonesia, Malaysia, Philippines, New Zealand, Thailand and Uruguay attended the meeting.

Representatives of the United States of America, Japan and the European Communities were present at the meeting as observers.

A keynote address was given by the Prime Minister of Australia, Mr. Bob Hawke. His address highlighted the destruction in agricultural markets and the hardship caused to farmers in non-subsidising agricultural exporting countries by the production and trade policies of the European Comnmunity, the United States and Japan. He noted that the welfare of the fair trading nations was being further jeopardised by the senseless trade war between the USA and the European Community and that credibility of the multilateral trading system itself was now in danger.

Mr. Hawke called for a halt to the predatory trade policies of the major industrialised countries and for concerted action by the fair trading nations to ensure that the liberalisation of agricultural trade was high on the agenda for the new round of multilateral trade negotiations expected to be launched at Punta del Este, Uruguay, in September 1986.

DECLARATION

Ministers agreed that there was an urgent need to reform and liberalise agricultural trade so as to improve the economic prospects of all participating countries.

Ministers noted that there was growing recognition of the agricultural trade crisis and its crippling effects on the economies of agricultural exporters, notably debtor nations, whose ability to service their debt was being continuously eroded. This recognition was reflected in the undertakings given at the Tokyo summit of seven industrialised countries in May 1986 to work towards a resolution of the problems created in world agricultural markets by their inappropriate domestic policies. Ministers welcomed the agreement in the Tokyo communiqué on the importance of adjustment policies. They expressed the firm view that this could be achieved in agriculture only by a programme of market liberalisation including a marked reduction in use of agricultural subsidies.

Ministers emphasised the importance of the MTN negotiations addressing agricultural trade issues as a high priority. In this context they undertook to seek the removal of market access barriers, substantial reductions of agricultural subsidies and the elimination within an agreed period, of subsidies affecting agricultural trade.

Ministers expressed the view that the preparations made in Geneva to develop a draft ministerial declaration to launch a new round of negotiations had achieved progress in several areas and reflected many of the concerns which needed to be addressed. Deficiencies remain, however, including the inadequate treatment of agricultural subsidies and the lack of a specific reference to domestic agricultural adjustment policies.

Ministers noted that, at Punta del Este, the draft declaration would be subject to discussion and decision at ministerial level for the first time. In that context they endorsed the need for a strong commitment to give a high priority to resolving the long-standing issues in agriculture and tropical products.

Ministers seriously questioned the value of a new round which failed to solve the long-standing problems in agricultural trade.

Ministers decided that they would meet in Punta del Este prior to the GATT ministerial meeting to ensure that their concerns regarding the negotiating objectives on agriculture are adequately met. This would be done by their seeking improvements in the declaration adopted so that there would be sufficient commitment to agricultural trade reform and liberalisation.

Ministers also considered that the commitments on standstill and rollback would be a litmus test of the good faith of all countries in joining the negotiations. They expressed the view that the standstill and rollback commitments should specifically cover all areas of trade in goods, including agriculture, and that appropriate multilateral surveillance should be implemented to that end.

Ministers agreed that they would meet regularly following the launch of the negotiations to oversee the progress of negotiations and to ensure that the problems of world agricultural trade remain high on the agenda for international action.

In view of the time that would be taken for the MTN process to achieve substantial results, ministers agreed that additional efforts were needed. These included pressure to secure early changes in current domestic farm support policies of those countries whose policies adversely affect international trade in agricultural products. Bilateral, regional and joint co-operative efforts would be considered.

Ministers agreed that the fair trading nations should expand their contact with developing country economic and regional groups, especially those with a focus on agricultural issues.

Ministers also agreed that while the GATT negotiations were underway the causes of and solutions to the current crisis in agricultural trade should be at the forefront of consideration in all relevant international fora such as the IMF, World Bank, OECD, FAO, UNCTAD and UNGA.

Ministers were convinced that such wide-ranging efforts were essential in view of the widespread misery and destruction being caused to efficient farmers around the world.

Ministers welcomed the presence at the conference of the observers from the United States, Japan and European Community, in view of their economic importance and shared responsibility for the reform of the international trade system.

In particular they welcomed the statement by the observer from the United States that the United States objectives in the negotiations will include "The phase out of all export subsidies affecting trade in agricultural products".

Ministers expressed their intention to continue the dialogue on these issues during the course of the negotiations.

Ministers expressed their appreciation for the contributions of farm industry representatives from Argentina, Australia, Canada and New Zealand in the formulation of strategies for agricultural trade reform. They agreed with the industry representatives that these exchanges should be continued and expanded as part of the future consultations among the fair trading nations.

Ministers congratulated the government of Australia for its initiative in convening this meeting. They expressed their gratitude for the warm hospitality extended to them.

APPENDIX 6

CHAIRMAN'S SUMMARY OF THE DISCUSSIONS ON THE PROBLEM OF DISEQUILIBRIA IN WORLD TRADE (BALANCE OF BENEFITS)

1.   There has been a proposal for the inclusion among the objectives of the negotiations that of redressing growing disequilibria in world trade and of achieving, in the spirit of the preamble to the General Agreement, a greater mutuality of advantages.

2.   However, it has been represented that the foregoing proposal might lead to a trading system incompatible with the basic objectives and principles of GATT, the guarantor of the open and non-discriminatory trading system.

3.   Nevertheless it was common ground that growing disequilibria in world trade constituted a serious problem and will need to be tackled by the countries concerned by various policy means including macro-economic policy, exchange rates, structural reform and trade policy.

4.   It was furthermore agreed that in the negotiations each and every contracting party should make genuine efforts to ensure mutual advantage and increased benefits to all participants, in accordance with the principles of the GATT.

APPENDIX 7

URUGUAY ROUND – NEGOTIATING GROUPS & CHAIRMEN

1. Tariffs	*Mr Lindsay Duthia* (Australia)
2. Non-Tariff Measures	Ambassador and Australian Special Trade
3. Natural Resource-Based Products	Representative, Europe
4. Textiles and Clothing	
5. Agriculture	*Mr. Aart de Zeeuw* (EC/Netherlands) Director-General of Agriculture, The Netherlands
6. Tropical Products	*Mr. Paul Leon Khee Seong* (Malaysia) MP, Former Minister of Primary Industries, Malaysia Vice-Chairman: *Mr. Siaka Coulibaly* (Côte d'Ivoire) Ambassador, Advisor to the Minister of Foreign Affairs, Côte d'Ivoire
7. GATT Articles	*Mr. John M. Weekes* (Canada) Director-General of Trade Policy, Department of External Affairs, Canada
8. MTN Agreements and Arrangements	*Dr. Chulsu Kim* (Korea) Assistant Minister of Trade, Ministry of Trade and Industry, Republic of Korea
9. Safeguards	*Mr. Georges A. Maciel* (Brazil) Ambassador, Permanent Representative of Brazil to the United Nations, New York
10. Subsidies and Countervailing Measures	*Mr. Michael D. Cartland* (Hong Kong) Permanent Representative of Hong Kong to GATT
11. Trade-Related Aspects of Intellectual Property Rights, including Trade in Counterfeit Goods	*Mr. Lars E.R. Anell* (Sweden) Ambassador, Permanent Representative of Sweden to the United Nations, Geneva
12. Trade-Related Investment Measures	*Mr. Tomohiko Kobayashi* (Japan) Ambassador, Special Economic Advisor to the Minister of Foreign Affairs, Japan
13. Dispute Settlement	*Mr. Julio Lacarte-Muro* (Uruguay) Ambassador, Permanent Representative of Uruguay to the GATT
14. Functioning of the GATT System	*Mr. Julius L. Katz* (United States) Former Assistant Secretary of State, United States
Surveillance Body	Chairman: *Mr. Madan G. Mathur* Deputy Director-General, GATT

APPENDIX 8

GUIDANCE DOCUMENTS FOR THE NEGOTIATIONS

PROPOSED STATEMENTS BY TNC CHAIRMAN ON THE MECHANISM FOR SURVEILLANCE OF STANDSTILL AND ROLLBACK

Chairman's Understanding on the Surveillance Mechanism Concerning Rollback Undertakings
"It is my understanding that participants maintaining measures that may be subject to the rollback commitment shall inform the Surveillance Body by 31 December 1987 of rollback undertakings resulting from the first round of consultations under paragraph 5."

Chairman's Understanding Regarding Paragraph 7 of Surveillance Text
"It is the understanding of the Chairman that the relevant GATT practice is the one followed by the GATT Council. The Council meets at periodic intervals, but if a contracting party considers that a matter cannot wait for the next regular meeting of the Council and requires urgent consideration, it may request a meeting for this purpose. When such requests have been made, they have normally been met, once the Chairman has consulted with interested parties."

Chairman's Understanding Regarding the Date of the First Meeting of the Surveillance Body
"It is the understanding of the Chairman that the first meeting of the Surveillance body will take place in the week beginning 23 February 1987."

GROUP NEGOTIATIONS ON SERVICES

DRAFT
PROGRAMME FOR THE INITIAL PHASE OF NEGOTIATIONS
Report by the Chairman
Discussions in the Group have focused on the initial phase of negotiations and on identifying a number of elements which should be addressed in 1987 in conformity with the negotiating objectives. These elements are listed below. It is understood that this list is non-exhaustive, and that no particular significance attaches to the way in which the items are formulated; there will be opportunity to give greater precision to their content in due course. It is also understood that neither the formulation of the items nor the order in which they are listed prejudge the relative importance of any of them, or imply any ordering for negotiating purposes.

Negotiating objectives
"Negotiations in this area shall aim to establish a multilateral framework of principles and rules for trade in services, including elaboration of possible disciplines for individual sectors, with a view to expansion of such trade under conditions of transparency and progressive liberalization and as a means of promoting economic growth of all trading partners and the development of developing countries. Such framework shall respect the policy objectives of national laws and regulations applying to services and shall take into account the work of relevant international organizations."

Elements
- Definitional and statistical issues
- Broad concepts on which principles and rules for trade in services, including possible disciplines for individual sectors, might be based
- Coverage of the multilateral framework for trade in services
- Existing international disciplines and arrangements
- Measures and practices contributing to or limiting the expansion of trade in services, including specifically any barriers perceived by individual participants, to which the conditions of transparency and progressive liberalization might be applicable

NON-TARIFF MEASURES
Negotiating Plan

Negotiating Objective
"Negotiations shall aim to reduce or eliminate non-tariff measures, including quantitative restrictions, without prejudice to any action to be taken if fulfilment of the rollback commitments."

Principal stages of the negotiating process
Initial Phase
- A first examination of the issues to be covered, including the relationship between the negotiations in this area and other areas of the negotiations. Establishment of an adequate data base for negotiation. Participants would also present proposals setting out the particular problems that they want to address and the techniques which they consider should be used to deal with them (bilateral, plurilateral or multilateral). Paper by the secretariat on the data base and relevant work already undertaken in the GATT on techniques for negotiating on quantitative restrictions and other non-tariff measures.
- The proposals by participants would be examined with a view to reaching a common understanding on appropriate techniques and procedures (bilateral requests and offers, subject to procedures to ensure transparency; multilateral approaches) and on subjects to be dealt with multilaterally.

Subsequent Negotiating Process
- Tabling of detailed requests for bilateral or plurilateral negotiations on specific measures and of specific texts relating to any issues to be dealt with multilaterally.
- Negotiations will proceed on the common basis.

Mechanism for Surveillance of Standstill and Rollback

The GNG recommends that the TNC decide to establish a mechanism as designated below for the surveillance of standstill and rollback commitments contained in Section C of Part I of the Ministerial Declaration:

Standstill
1. Any participant may bring to the attention of a Surveillance Body, open to all participants, through the GATT secretariat, any action or measure, taken by itself or

another participant, which it believes relevant to the fulfilment of the standstill commitments. Any such notification will be deemed to have been submitted to the Surveillance Body upon its receipt by the secretariat.

2. The secretariat shall circulate promptly to all participants, and in no case later than 10 working days after receipt, a copy of all notifications addressed to the Surveillance Body. When notifications relate to actions by other participants (reverse notifications) the secretariat shall promptly inform the country to which they relate. Any comments[1] and any other relevant factual material received within the above period of 10 working days will be circulated together with the notification. If any comments or further information become available subsequently they will be circulated promptly.

3. The Surveillance Body will examine the relationship between the actions or measures notified and paragraphs (i), (ii), and (iii) of the standstill commitment contained in Section C of Part I of the Ministerial Declaration at its first meeting following the 10 working day period referred to in paragraph 2 above. The Surveillance Body will transmit a record of its proceedings to the next meeting of the TNC. (This record will be transmitted to the GNG for its information.)

Rollback

4. Any participant may bring to the attention of other participants, through the GATT secretariat, measures which it is applying or measures applied by another participant, which it believes should be subject to the rollback commitment. It will be open to any participant to notify to the Surveillance Body any omission by another participant which it believes to be relevant to the fulfilment of the rollback commitment.

5 Participants concerned shall consult in order to arrive at rollback undertakings. Timely notice of such consultations shall be sent to the secretariat for the information cf all participants so that any affected participants may also take part in consultations if they so wish. Participants shall notify any undertakings resulting from these consultations to the Surveillance Body.

6. The Surveillance Body shall monitor the implementation of the undertakings resulting from the consultations referred to in paragraph 5 above and report to the TNC. (This report will be transmitted to the GNG for its information.)

7. In order to carry out the functions set out above, the Surveillance Body will meet at least three times a year. It may also meet at the request of any participant, in accordance with the usual GATT practices.

8. The TNC will meet at least every six months to carry out, on the basis of the records and reports transmitted to it by the Surveillance Body, a periodic evaluation of the implementation of the standstill and rollback commitments, and of its impact on the process of multilateral trade negotiations and in relation to the interests of individual participants.

---

[1] The absence of comments by a country subject to a reverse notification shall not be deemed to constitute an admission that the measure is subject to the standstill commitment.

NATURAL RESOURCE-BASED PRODUCTS
Negotiating Plan

Negotiating Objective

"Negotiations shall aim to achieve the fullest liberalization of trade in natural resource-based products including in their processed and semi-processed forms. The negotiations shall aim to reduce or eliminate tariff and non-tariff measures, including tariff escalation."

Principal stages of the negotiating process
Initial Phase

- Determination of issues relevant to the Negotiating Objective taking into account documentation established by the Working Party on Natural Resource-Based Products and proposals by participants.

- Establishment of a factual basis for negotiations.

- Elaboration of techniques and modalities for achieving the agreed objectives of negotiations in this area, taking into account those elaborated in other relevant areas.

- Establishment of a common negotiating basis.

Subsequent Negotiating Process

- Tabling of requests and offers.

- Negotiations will proceed on the common basis.

DECISION ON "NEGOTIATING STRUCTURE"

In carrying out the programme of negotiations contained in Part I of the Punta del Este Declaration, the GNG shall discharge its functions in strict accordance with the provisions of Section G thereof, and will meet as frequently as necessary.

AGRICULTURE
Negotiating Plan

Negotiating Objective

"CONTRACTING PARTIES agree that there is an urgent need to bring more discipline and predictability to world agricultural trade by correcting and preventing restrictions and distortions including those related to structural surpluses so as to reduce the uncertainty, imbalances and instability in world agricultural markets.

Negotiations shall aim to achieve greater liberalization of trade in agriculture and bring all measures affecting import access and export competition under strengthened and more operationally effective GATT rules and disciplines, taking into account the general principles governing the negotiations, by:

(i) improving market access through, *inter alia*, the reduction of import barriers;

(ii) improving the competitive environment by increasing discipline on the use of all direct and indirect subsidies and other measures affecting directly or indirectly agricultural trade, including the phased reduction of their negative effects and dealing with their causes;

(iii)   minimizing the adverse effects that sanitary and phytosanitary regulations and barriers can have on trade in agriculture, taking into account the relevant international agreements.

In order to achieve the above objectives, the negotiating group having primary responsibility for all aspects of agriculture will use the Recommendations adopted by the CONTRACTING PARTIES at their Fortieth Session, which were developed in accordance with the GATT 1982 Ministerial Programme, and take account of the approaches suggested in the work of the Committee on Trade in Agriculture without prejudice to other alternatives that might achieve the objectives of the negotiations."

TARIFFS
Negotiating Plan

Negotiating Objective
"Negotiations shall aim, by appropriate methods, to reduce or, as appropriate, eliminate tariffs including the reduction or elimination of high tariffs and tariff escalation. Emphasis shall be given to the expansion of the scope of tariff concessions among all participants."

Principal stages of the negotiating process
Initial Phase
- Submission of proposals by participants on:
- a tariff-cutting approach/approaches, including elimination of tariffs;
- the elimination or reduction of high tariffs and tariff escalation in appropriate product areas;
- possible criteria to expand the scope of tariff concessions including the degree of tariff bindings.
- Broadening and updating of factual basis (Tariff Study files, Harmonized System data bank).
- Factual notes by secretariat and/or participants, as required, on issues to be negotiated.

Subsequent Negotiating Process
- Agreement on a common negotiating basis comprising the issues listed under the Initial Phase above.
- Bilateral phase of the negotiations between participants on individual tariff items.
- Elaboration of a tariff protocol.

GATT ARTICLES
Negotiating Plan

Negotiating Objective
"Participants shall review existing GATT Articles, provisions and disciplines as requested by interested contracting parties, and, as appropriate, undertake negotiations."

Principal stages of the negotiating process
Initial Phase

• Requests by interested contracting parties for review of GATT Articles, provisions and disciplines, indicating why they consider that these should be the subject of negotiations. Factual background papers by the secretariat on these Articles, provisions and disciplines. Review, following requests by participants, of GATT Articles, provisions and disciplines, with a view to determining issues on which negotiations are appropriate.

Subsequent Negotiating Process

• Tabling of specific texts by contracting parties on issues so identified for negotiation. Review and analysis of these proposals.

• Negotiations on the basis established.

TROPICAL PRODUCTS
Negotiating Plan

Negotiating Objective

"Negotiations shall aim at the fullest liberalization of trade in tropical products, including in their processed and semi-processed forms and shall cover both tariff and all non-tariff measures affecting trade in these products.

The CONTRACTING PARTIES recognise the importance of trade in tropical products to a large number of less developed contracting parties and agree that negotiations in this area shall receive special attention, including the timing of the negotiations and the implementation of the results as provided for in B(ii)" of the Ministerial Declaration.

Principal stages of the negotiating process
Initial Phase

This phase would cover the following work:

(a) exchange of views on work done so far in GATT in this area;

(b) compilation of background material for negotiations;

(c) submission of initial proposals and other inputs by participants aimed at achieving the agreed objectives of negotiations in this area;

(d) agreement on techniques and modalities as a common basis for negotiations, including the tabling of initial requests/offers.

Subsequent Negotiating Process

Negotiations will proceed as early as possible in 1988 on the basis of the work in the previous phase with the aim of achieving concrete results and their implementation at the earliest possible date in the light of the provisions of Section B(ii) of the Ministerial Declaration.

Monitoring of Progress

Throughout the negotiations on tropical products special attention at the appropriate level will be given to the task of reviewing the progress achieved.

MTN AGREEMENTS AND ARRANGEMENTS
Negotiating Plan

Negotiating Objective

"Negotiations shall aim to improve, clarify, or expand, as appropriate, Agreements and Arrangements negotiated in the Tokyo Round of Multilateral Negotiations."

Principal stages of the negotiating process
Initial Phase

Suggestions by participants indicating the issues that they wish to raise with respect to individual MTN Agreements and Arrangements. Factual background paper by the Secretariat on these issues. Examination of the proposals made by participants, with a view to clarifying issues on which negotiations are appropriate, having regard to work in the relevant Committees and Councils established under the MTN Agreements and Arrangements. In the light of the issues identified, agreement on the negotiating techniques and modalities for the subsequent stages.

Subsequent Negotiating Process

- Submission of specific texts by interested participants on issues identified for negotiation. Review and analysis of the proposals.
- Negotiations on the basis established.

TEXTILES AND CLOTHING
Negotiating Plan

Negotiating Objective

"Negotiations in the area of textiles and clothing shall aim to formulate modalities that would permit eventual integration of this sector into GATT on the basis of strengthened GATT rules and disciplines, thereby also contributing to the objective of further liberalization of trade."

Principal stages of the negotiating process
Initial Phase

This phase will be devoted to preparatory work in this area. The annual reports of the TSB, information provided by the Sub-Committee on Adjustment and other sources, as well as material from the Working Party on Textiles and Clothing including the related documentation as updated, can make a useful contribution to this stage of work.

Subsequent Negotiating Process

- Examination of techniques and modalities for achievement of the objectives set out in this area in the light of proposals made by participants.
- Negotiations aimed at achieving the Negotiating Objective in this area.

DISPUTE SETTLEMENT
Negotiating Plan

Negotiating Objective

"In order to ensure prompt and effective resolution of disputes to the benefit of all contracting parties, negotiations shall aim to improve and strengthen the rules and the procedures of the dispute settlement process, while recognizing the contribution that would be made by more effective and enforceable GATT rules and disciplines. Negotiations shall include the development of adequate arrangements for overseeing and monitoring of the procedures that would facilitate compliance with adopted recommendations."

Principal stages of the negotiating process
Initial Phase

* Submission by participants of their analyses of the functioning of the GATT dispute settlement process and of their views on matters to be taken up in the negotiations. Factual background papers by the Secretariat as required. Review of the dispute settlement process with a view to identifying issues on which negotiations are appropriate.

Tabling of specific proposals by participants on issues identified for negotiation.

Subsequent Negotiating Process

* Review and analysis of proposals.

* Negotiations on the basis established.

Principal stages of the negotiating process
Initial Phase

Identification of major problems and their causes, including all measures affecting directly or indirectly agricultural trade, taking into account *inter alia* work done by the CTA, and elaboration of an indicative list of issues considered relevant by participants to achieving the Negotiating Objective.

The concurrent submission of supplementary information on measures and policies affecting trade in the AG/FOR-series, including full notification of all direct and indirect subsidies and other measures affecting directly or indirectly agricultural trade.

Consideration of basic principles to govern world trade in agriculture.

Submission and initial examination of proposals by participants aimed at achieving the Negotiating Objective.

Subsequent Negotiating Process

Within this process, further examination as appropriate of proposals and initiation of negotiations.

Negotiations with a view to reaching agreement on (a) comprehensive texts of strengthened and more operationally effective GATT rules and disciplines; (b) the nature and the content of specific multilateral commitments to be undertaken including as appropriate implementation programmes and transitional arrangements; (c) any other understandings which should also be deemed necessary for the fulfilment of the Negotiating Objective; and (d) exchange of concessions, as appropriate.

TRADE-RELATED INVESTMENT MEASURES
Negotiating Plan

Negotiating Objective
"Following an examination of the operation of GATT Articles related to the trade restrictive and distorting effects of investment measures, negotiations should elaborate, as appropriate, further provisions that may be necessary to avoid such adverse effects on trade."

Principal stages of the negotiating process
Initial Phase

Identification and examination of the operation of GATT Articles related to the trade restrictive and distorting effects of investment measures, on the basis of submissions by participants and with the assistance, as appropriate, of background documentation by the secretariat.

Subsequent Negotiating Process

● Definition of areas in which negotiations may be required to elaborate, as appropriate, further provisions that may be necessary to avoid restrictive and distorting effects of investment measures on trade, on the basis of proposals by participants.

● Negotiations on the basis established.

SAFEGUARDS
Negotiating Plan

Negotiating Objective

"(i)   A comprehensive agreement on safeguards is of particular importance to the strengthening of the GATT system and to progress in the Multilateral Trade Negotiations.

(ii)   The agreement on safeguards:

● shall be based on the basic principles of the General Agreement;

● shall contain, *inter alia,* the following elements: transparency, coverage, objective criteria for action including the concept of serious injury or threat thereof, temporary nature, degressivity and structural adjustment, compensation and retaliation, notification, consultation, multilateral surveillance and dispute settlement; and

● shall clarify and reinforce the disciplines of the General Agreement and should apply to all contracting parties."

Negotiating Process

● Examination of the issues in this area would be carried out with the assistance of papers by participants setting out their specific suggestions for achieving the negotiating objective in this area, and of a paper by the secretariat on relevant work already undertaken in the GATT, including in particular on the elements enumerated in the Ministerial Declaration, and any other factual background material as required.

● Proposals by participants would be examined with a view to drawing up a draft text of a comprehensive agreement as a basis for negotiation.

● Negotiations will proceed on the basis of the draft text with a view to drawing up and concluding a comprehensive agreement as expeditiously as possible, taking into account that such an agreement is of particular importance to the strengthening of the GATT system and to progress in the Multilateral Trade Negotiations.

FUNCTIONING OF THE GATT SYSTEM
Negotiating Plan

Negotiating Objectives
"Negotiations shall aim to develop understandings and arrangements:
(i) to enhance the surveillance in the GATT to enable regular monitoring of trade policies and practices of contracting parties and their impact on the functioning of the multilateral trading system;
(ii) to improve the overall effectiveness and decision-making of the GATT as an institution, including, *inter alia,* through involvement of Ministers;
(iii) to increase the contribution of the GATT to achieving greater coherence in global economic policy-making through strengthening its relationship with other international organizations responsible for monetary and financial matters."

Principal stages of the negotiating process
Initial Phase
- a first examination of issues on the basis of proposals by participants;

- any background documentation required from the secretariat;

Subsequent Negotiating Process
- Establishment of common working texts on which to base any understandings and arrangements which are to be negotiated.

- In this stage final texts will be agreed upon as appropriate, containing understandings or specifying arrangements relating to those aspects of the functioning of the GATT system referred to in section E of the Ministerial Declaration.

TRADE-RELATED ASPECTS OF INTELLECTUAL PROPERTY RIGHTS, INCLUDING TRADE IN COUNTERFEIT GOODS
Negotiating Plan

Negotiating Objective
"In order to reduce the distortions and impediments to international trade, and taking into account the need to promote effective and adequate protection of intellectual property rights, and to ensure that measures and procedures to enforce intellectual property rights do not themselves become barriers to legitimate trade, the negotiations shall aim to clarify GATT provisions and elaborate as appropriate new rules and disciplines.

Negotiations shall aim to develop a multilateral framework of principles, rules and disciplines dealing with international trade in counterfeit goods, taking into account work already undertaken in the GATT.

These negotiations shall be without prejudice to other complementary initiatives that may be taken in the World Intellectual Property Organization and elsewhere to deal with these matters."

Principal stages of the negotiating process
Initial Phase

- Trade-related aspects of intellectual property rights: Identification of relevant GATT provisions and examination of their operation on the basis of suggestions by participants for achieving the Negotiating Objective and of factual information by the secretariat as required. Initial examination of the specific suggestions and of the procedures and techniques that might be used to implement them.

- Trade in counterfeit goods: Examination of the matters to be dealt with in this area on the basis of the report of the Group of Experts (L/5878), of other work already undertaken in the GATT and of papers by participants setting out their suggestions for achieving the negotiating objectives. Other factual information as required.

- Consideration of the relationship between the negotiations in this area and initiatives in other form. Collection of information from relevant sources.

Subsequent Negotiating Process

- If necessary, further examination of the specific suggestions and of the procedures and techniques that might be used to implement them.

- Tabling of specific texts by interested participants, as appropriate. Examination of these texts with a view to establishment of a common negotiating basis.

- Negotiations on the basis established.

GNG CHAIRMAN'S STATEMENT
REGARDING THE NEGOTIATING PLANS

"Wherever the words "Negotiating Objective" appear under the "Principal stages of the negotiating process" of the Negotiating Plans, they refer to the entire text which appears under the heading "Negotiating Objective" at the beginning of each plan."

SUBSIDIES AND COUNTERVAILING MEASURES
Negotiating Plan

Negotiating Objective

"Negotiations on subsidies and countervailing measures shall be based on a review of Articles VI and XVI and the MTN Agreement on subsidies and countervailing measures with the objective of improving GATT disciplines relating to all subsidies and countervailing measures that affect international trade. A negotiating group will be established to deal with these issues."

Principal stages of the negotiating process
Initial Phase

Submission of proposals by participants, together with any background notes, on issues to be taken up in the negotiations, and on negotiating techniques. Factual background notes by the secretariat. Examination of the proposals and the documentation.

Subsequent Negotiating Process

- Development of a common negotiating basis for improving GATT disciplines relating to all subsidies and countervailing measures that affect international trade. Tabling of specific drafting proposals by participants.
- Negotiations on the basis of specific drafting proposals.

STATEMENT BY THE CHAIRMAN OF THE GNG ON NEGOTIATING STRUCTURE AND CHAIRMANSHIP

It is my understanding that the Decision on the Negotiating Structure has been adopted on the basis of the following understanding:

1. Meetings of the Negotiating Groups will be arranged in the year 1987 on the calendar pattern set out in the Decision on the Negotiating Structure.

2. Each of the 14 Negotiating Groups will have its own chairman and will operate as a separate entity.

3. It will be open to two or more Negotiating Groups to hold joint meetings if they so decide.

4. A given person may be appointed to the chairmanship of more than one Negotiating Group.

5. It is envisaged that, subject to agreement on the persons in question, the same individual may be appointed for the initial phase to the chairmanships of Negotiating Groups 1, 2, 3 and 4. The same approach would be considered for Groups 7 and 8 and for Groups 13 and 14.

6. A meeting of Heads of Delegation to the GNG, to be held before 9 February, will approve a list of persons to be appointed as chairmen of the Groups.

SUMMARY OF MAJOR PROVISIONS OF US TRADE BILL, 1988

Unfair Trade Practices

The administration will be required to begin investigations into countries that maintain numerous and pervasive unfair trade barriers. The authority to initiate such "301" cases is transferred to the U.S. trade representative from the president, as is the formal authority to order retaliation. Lawmakers noted, however, that the trade representative serves at the direction of the president and is unlikely to take action he opposes.

The legislation would give the administration some discretion in deciding whether to retaliate and how.

Import Relief

There are several significant changes governing federal relief to domestic industries hurt by imports. Industries that currently can qualify for relief merely by showing they are seriously injured by increasing imports will, under the trade bill, also have to show that they are prepared to make a "positive adjustment" to import competition. This means that a dying industry couldn't win relief unless it demonstrated it could become competitive again.

Congress decided to give the administration some discretion in deciding when to grant import relief, permitting relief in ways other than imposing tariffs or quotas on the offending imports. Earlier versions of the trade bill would have required the administration to take action once substantial injury was found. But Congress added a provision saying the administration wouldn't be forced to act if, for example, any action would result in greater economic and social costs than benefits.

The measure also trims or eliminates U.S. duties on a number of products for which there is no source in this country.

Trade Negotiations

The bill grants the executive branch special authority to negotiate in the Uruguay Round of world trade talks now under way and expected to end in 1990. If the next president submits a new world trade pact for ratification by May 31, 1991, Congress will consider it under an expedited system that guarantees quick consideration without amendments.

In general, the administration gets the authority to slash duties as much as 50% as part of the Uruguay Round negotiations.

The bill also grants U.S. approval to a new agreement for harmonizing the system by which countries categorize goods in world trade. This system is designed to make statistics more reliable.

Foreign Takeovers

The president gets the power to block foreign investments that impair U.S. national security. But he can act only if existing review procedures show that an acquisition threatens national scurity and if the current procedures can't derail or reshape the acquisition. Further, the president can block an acquisition under the trade bill only if no other law – including antitrust, environmental and defense procurement acts – can stop it. And the president must cite credible evidence that the foreign party involved is likely to take action that will impair national security.

Dumping

The bill doesn't make major changes in current law covering countervailing duties and dumping. It establishes as a U.S. negotiating goal in trade talks the banning of "diversionary input dumping" – cases in which finished products imported into the U.S. include materials that were dumped in the country where the finished goods were made. Dumping is selling a product in a foreign market at less than the home-market price or the cost of production.

Countervailing duties are aimed at combatting foreign subsidies.

The bill authorizes the Commerce Department to ask other countries to bring their own dumping cases where dumped components are used in finished products sold in the U.S. And to prevent multinational corporations from masking dumping by manipulating prices that various subsidiaries charge each other, the bill authorizes the department to disregard intra-company transfer prices in figuring dumping and to use costs of production instead. It also establishes a method for calculating whether countries with state-run economies are dumping goods in the U.S.

Export Controls

Congress voted to abolish controls on the export of many widely available electronics products to Japan and 14 North Atlantic Treaty Organization allies. Since these products, which include personal computers, are subject only to routine licensing, decontrolling this category is expected to reduce paperwork and improve delivery times.

The bill also clarifies the Pentagon's role in reviewing licenses for exports to non-communist countries, stating that the review should be done only for "national security" reasons. Some members of Congress have complained that the Pentagon sometimes blocks U.S. exports on foreign-policy grounds that go beyond its legislative mandate.

Securities Dealers

The legislation bars foreign companies from serving as primary dealers in U.S. government securities unless their governments reciprocate.

The measure is aimed primarily at Japan, and it would force three big Japanese securities firms out of the prestigious business of being primary dealers in U.S. government securities – if Japan doesn't offer U.S. companies within one year the "same competitive opportunites" Japanese firms enjoy for dealing in that country's government securities.

The Japanese primary dealers that could be affected by the provisio are the U.S. units of Nomura Securities Co., Nikko Securities Co. and Daiwa Securities Co. The provision would exempt primary dealers controlled by, or being acquired by, Industrial Bank of Japan Ltd., Sanwa Bank Ltd. It would also exempt First Boston Corp., in which Credit Suisse has a major holding.

Primary dealers are elite institutions that deal directly with the Federal Reserve Bank of New York when it buys and sells government securities as part of its open-market operations. Some large institutional investors will do business only with primary dealers.

Agriculture

Through the fiscal year ending Sept. 30, 1989, the bill provides $2.5 billion for boosting exports of farm products. This program, aimed at the European Community, subsidizes U.S. farm exports to countries that subsidize their own farm products.

Toshiba Sanctions

The bill bars all imports from Japan's Toshiba Machine Co. for three years in retaliation for that company's illegal sale to the Soviet Union of sophisticated machine tools useful for making submarines quieter. The bill penalizes the parent Toshiba Corp. with a three-year ban on doing business with U.S. government agencies. Toshiba Corp would save most of its U.S. sales of about $2.5 billion a year, but its subisidiary could lose as much as $300 million over the three-year period, according to legislative estimates.

Federal agencies don't have to honor the Toshiba ban on existing contracts or on items for which Toshiba is the only source.

The bill also prescribes sanctions for foreign companies that commit similar violations in the future. Companies that "knowingly" breach export-control rules could be subject to a two-year to five-year ban on U.S. sales and federal contracting. However, parents of subsidiaries guilty of these violations could be exempted if their governments have a good record of enforcing export regulations and if the parents maintain effective internal controls.

Windfall Profits

The windfall profits tax on domestically produced crude oil is repealed. The tax was designed to capture for the government some of the profits generated when controls were lifted from soaring oil prices in 1980. The repeal, according to proponents, won't result in any lost revenue for the government because oil prices are currently below the level at which companies have to pay anything.

Worker Retraining

One section authorizes $980 million for retraining workers displaced by plant closings or modernization. Workers would be eligible even if their job losses didn't result from imports.

The legislation also expands the assistance programs for workers displaced by imports. It attempts to move from the current cash-benefits program to one of promoting adjustment by making enrollment in retraining programs a condition of receiving benefits. The president is authorized to impose a small import fee to pay for the benefits.

Intellectual Property

The president is directed to act against countries that permit piracy of U.S."intellectual property." He must identify countries that don't protect copyrights and patents and initiate expedited unfair-trade investigations in the most egregious cases. The president may decline to act if doing so would be against the national economic interest.

Holders of patents on processes by which products are made, as in the biotechnology and pharmaceutical industries, will be allowed to sue U.S. importers of any products that use their patented processes in a foreign country where the patents aren't protected. Currently, patent-process holders can seek to prevent such products from coming into the U.S., but can't recover damages.

Another provision eliminates a requirement that U.S. patent holders prove they are injured before they can obtain government orders banning imports of products that infringe their patents.

Telecommunications

The president will be required to negotiate with foreign countries to win greater access to their markets for U.S. makers of telecommunications equipment. The provision directs the president to use as leverage in such talks the threat that foreign companies' access to the U.S. telecommunications market could be denied if foreign governments don't reduce barriers to U.S. companies.

Anti-Bribery Laws

The 1977 law against corporate bribery of foreign officials is clarified as to what kind of knowledge would make corporate officials liable for bribes made by employees or agents. A U.S. company will be liable for employee violations if top officials ignored indications of improper actions taken on the company's behalf.

The current Foreign Corrupt Practices Act allows so-called grease payments to facilitate certain activities such as unloading goods on foreign docks. The trade bill clarifies permissible payments to include reasonable expenses, such as for travel and lodging, associated with selling goods overseas.

Exchange Rates

The bill puts into legislative language current U.S. policies on exchange rates and international economic policy co-ordination. It requires the U.S. to hold multilateral talks with other major nations to improve both co-ordination of economic policies and existing mechanisms for stabilizing exchange rates. In addition, the U.S. must hold talks on exchange rates with any country that runs trade surpluses with the U.S. and the rest of the world and that the U.S. believes is manipulating its exchange rates. Annual reports to Congress would be required on how the two types of talks are going.

Third World Debt

The Treasury secretary is directed to open discussions with other countries on the possibility of creating a special "debt facility" – an entity that could purchase Third World debt, swap it, convert it into securities or otherwise act to reduce the debtor countries' debt load. However, the legislation gives the secretary an escape clause by which he can avoid holding such talks, which are opposed by the Reagan adminsitration. The Treasury won't have to conduct the talks if an interim study concludes that such talks would carry a "material risk" of reducing the value of the debt, disrupting debt service, or causing defaults. A final study is required within 12 months of the bill's passage, when a new president will be in office.

The bill also would require the U.S. to ask the World Bank and International Monetary Fund to do new studies examining all the proposed debt-problem solutions.

Competitiveness

The bill attempts to strengthen the Commerce Department's data collection by combining two of its existing data banks – one that identifies export opportunties and another designed as a policy-making tool – into a "national trade data bank." The retooled facility could help US. companies compete for overseas sales.

Sources: "Senate Approves Major Trade Measures by Vote of 85-11 and Sends it to Reagan," Wall Street Journal, August 4, 1988, p.3; reprinted by permission.

ELEMENTS OF A CANADA-UNITED STATES FREE TRADE AGREEMENT

SYNOPSIS

On October 3, 1987, Canada and the United States agreed in principle on the elements to be included in a free-trade agreement. These elements will be transformed into the actual legal text of the Agreement over the course of the next three weeks. A synopsis of the elements that have been agreed follows.

Objectives and Scope

The two governments have agreed to establish a free-trade area agreement between them pursuant to the provisions of Article XXIV of the General Agreement on Tariffs and Trade with the following objectives:

- to eliminate barriers to trade in goods and services;

- to establish predictable rules, secure access and fair competition;

- to reduce significantly impediments to cross-border investment;

- to establish effective procedures and institutions for the joint administration of the Agreement and the resolution of disputes; and

- to lay the foundation for further bilateral and multilateral co-operation to expand and enhance the benefits of the Agreement.

The agreement will cover trade in goods and services and investment and involve federal, state and provincial measures.

Tariffs and Rules of Origin

The two governments have agreed to remove all tariffs by January 1, 1998. Tariffs will be eliminated on the basis of three formulas:

- some will be eliminated on the agreement entering into force on January 1, 1989;

- some will be eliminated in five equal steps, most starting on January 1, 1989; and

- some wil be eliminated in ten steps, most starting on January 1, 1989.

Goods which originate in Canada and the United States will qualify for the new tariff treatment. For goods incorporating offshore raw materials or components, it has been agreed that goods qualify for treatment as either of U.S. or Canadian origin if they have been sufficiently changed either in Canada or the United States to be classified differently than the raw materials or components from which they are made. The governments will use the tariff classification of the Harmonized System now being implemented by both governments. In certain cases, goods will need to incur a certain percentage of manufacturing cost in the country of origin.

Customs Matters

The two governments have agreed that:

- duty drawbacks and similar programs on goods imported from other countries, including through U.S. Foreign Trade Zones, will be eliminated for bilateral trade after January 1, 1994;

- neither party will introduce new duty waivers tied to specific performance requirements. All existing duty waivers will be eliminated by January 1, 1998; and

- customs user fees will be phased out on bilateral trade by January 1, 1993.

Quantitative Restrictions

Both parties have agreed to maintain the basic rules of GATT to regulate quantitative restrictions on imports or exports. Existing quantitative restrictions will be eliminated, either immediately or according to a timetable, or grandfathered.

Trade Remedies and Dispute Settlement

The two governments have agreed to a unique dispute settlement mechanism which guarantees the impartial application of their respective anti-dumping and countervailing duty laws and other aspects of trade remedy law. Either government may seek a review of an anti-dumping or countervailing duty determination by a bilateral panel with binding powers. Concurrently, the two governments will work towards establishing a new regime to address problems of dumping and subsidization to come into effect at the end of the seventh year.

Additionally, the two governments have agreed that changes in anti-dumping and countervailing duty legislation apply to each other only following consultation and if specifically provided for in the new legislation. Moreover, either government may ask a bilateral panel to review such changes in light of the object and purpose of the agreement and their rights and obligations under the GATT Anti-dumping and Subsidies Codes. Should a panel recommend modifications, the parties will consult on such modifications. Failure to reach agreement gives the other party the right to take comparable legislative or equivalent executive action or terminate the agreement.

Emergency Measures

The two governments have agreed to more stringent standards for the application of emergency safeguards (quotas or surcharges on imports causing serious injury) to bilateral trade. Except where the other Party is the major source of injury or is contributing importantly to the injury, they agree to exempt each other from safeguard measures. Bilaterally applied emergency measures are subject to compensation and protection against reductions below the trend line of previous bilateral trade.

Government Procurement

The two governments have agreed to expand access to purchases by governments by building on the GATT government procurement code. They have agreed to improved procedures for trade between them and to extend coverage of the Code to purchases between $25,000 U.S. and $171,000 U.S., the current threshold for coverage under the GATT Code.

National Treatment

The two governments have agreed to build on the GATT provision requiring that they will extend the same treatment to each other's goods as regards internal regulatory and fiscal requirements.

Technical Standards

The two governments have agreed to build on the GATT Standards Code. They will seek to harmonize federal standards and encourage harmonization at the state and provincial and private level.

Trade in Agricultural Goods

The two governments have agreed to a package of trade liberalizing measures for trade in agriculture including:

- eliminating all tariffs (but allowing Canada to restore temporarily tariffs on fresh fruits and vegetables for a twenty-year period under depressed price conditions);

- exempting each other from restrictions under their respective meat import laws;

- prohibition of export subsidies on bilateral trade;

- an exemption for Canada from any future quantitative import restrictions on products containing 10% or less sweetener and on grains and grain products; and

- conditional elimination of Canadian import licences for wheat, barley and oats and their products, and eliminating Canadian Western Grain Transportation subsidies on exports to the United States.

They will work with each other bilaterally and in the GATT to further improve and enhance trade in agriculture.

Wine and Distilled Spirits

The two governments have agreed to reduce barriers to trade in wine and distilled spirits. Beer is not covered in the agreement. They will eliminate discriminatory markups for spirits immediately and for wine over a period of seven years. All other discriminatory pricing measures will be eliminated immediately. They will also reduce discrimination in listing practices and extend national treatment to future changes in distribution systems.

Trade in Energy

They have agreed to eliminate a range of specific barriers to trade in energy (oil, gas, coal, electricity, uranium), including:

- all U.S. restrictions on enrichment of Canadian uranium; and

- the embargo on exports of Alaskan crude oil up to 50,000 barrels a day.

They have also agreed to ease regulatory restrictions on trade in energy products.

Automotive Trade

The two governments agreed to leave the Auto Pact intact. In order to provide for improved conditions of trade in automotive products, they have agreed:

- to eliminate all tariffs on automotive products within ten years;

- all vehicles will be subject to a special rule of origin creating new opportunities for production and employment in North America;

- to eliminate the duty remission programs by 1996; and

- to limit the duty-free entry privileges of the Auto Pact to current participants.

They have also agreed to establish a blue-ribbon panel to advise the two governments on automotive issues.

Trade in Services

The agreement will provide, for the first time, a set of disciplines covering a large number of service sectors. The agreement will provide that the two governments in future will extend the principles of national treatment, right of commercial presence and right of establishment to each other's providers of services. Additional sectoral annexes will clarify this general obligation with respect to transportation, enhanced telecommunications and computer services, tourism and architecture.

Temporary Entry for Business Purposes

The agreement will provide for improved and easier border crossing by business persons trading in goods and services.

Financial Services

The two governments have undertaken to grandfather existing privileges in each other's market and improve access and competition for financial institutions consistent with prudential and regulatory requirements. Additionally, Canadian banks in the United States will be able to underwrite Canadian government securities. Canadian financial institutions will be treated the same as U.S. banks with respect to any changes in the Glass-Steagall Act governing the relationship between the banking and securities industries.

Investment

The two governments have agreed in future to liberalize the treatment given to each other's investors with respect to:

- the establishment of new firms;
- the acquisition of existing firms; and
- the conduct, operation and sale of established firms.

Both governments retain the right to maintain existing measures not in conformity with these principles.

Canada retains the right to review the acquisition of firms in Canada by U.S. investors, but has agreed to phase in higher threshold levels for direct acquisition. The review of indirect acquisition will be phased out.

Cultural Industries

The government retains its full capacity to support cultural industries in Canada (film and video, music and sound recording, publishing and cable and broadcasting).

Institutional Provisions

The agreement will establish a bilateral Commission at the ministerial level to supervise the implementation and adminsitration of the agreement.

Notification and Consultation

The agreement will provide mandatory notification and consultation procedures to ensure the smooth operation of the agreement and to encourage the avoidance of disputes.

Dispute Settlement for Matters Other than Trade Remedies

The two governments have agreed to bi-national panel procedures at the instance of either party to make recommendations for the settlement of disputes regarding the interpretation and application of the agreement. By mutual agreement, they may also refer such disputes to binding interpretation.

Source: Trade: Securing Canada's Future, External Affairs, Canada, 1988.

Sponsoring Organisations

The British-North American Research Association was inaugurated in December 1969. Its primary purpose is to sponsor research on British-North American economic relations in association with the British-North American Committee. Publications of the British-North American Research Association as well as publications of the British-North American Committee are available from the Association's office, Grosvenor Gardens House, 35-37 Grosvenor Gardens, London SW1W 0BS (Tel. 01-828 6644). The Association is recognised as a charity and is governed by a Council under the chairmanship of A. B. Marshall.

The National Planning Association is an independent, private, nonprofit, nonpolitical organization that carries on research and policy formulation in the public interest. NPA was founded during the Great Depression of the 1930s when conflicts among the major economic groups—business, labor, agriculture—threatened to paralyze national decision making on the critical issues confronting American society. It was dedicated to the task of getting these diverse groups to work together to narrow areas of controversy and broaden areas of agreement and to provide on specific problems concrete programs for action planned in the best traditions of a functioning democracy. Such democratic planning, NPA believes, involves the development of effective governmental and private policies and programs not only by official agencies but also through the independent initiative and cooperation of the main private-sector groups concerned. And to preserve and strengthen American political and economic democracy, the necessary government actions have to be consistent with, and stimulate the support of, a dynamic private sector.

NPA brings together influential and knowledgeable leaders from business, labor, agriculture, and the applied and academic professions to serve on policy committees. These committees identify emerging problems confronting the nation at home and abroad and seek to develop and agree upon policies and programs for coping with them. The research and writing for these committees are provided by NPA's professional staff and, as required, by outside experts.

In addition, NPA's professional staff undertakes research designed to provide data and ideas for policymakers and planners in government and the private sector. These activities include the preparation on a regular basis of economic and demographic projections for the national economy, regions, states, metropolitan areas, and counties; research on national goals and priorities, productivity and economic growth, welfare and dependency problems, employment and manpower needs, and energy and environmental questions; analyses and forecasts of changing international realities and their implications for U.S. policies; and analyses of important new economic, social and political realities confronting American society.

NPA publications, including those of the British-North American Committee, can be obtained from the Association's office, 1616 P Street, N.W., Suite 400, Washington, D.C. 20036 (Tel. 202-265-7685).

The C. D. Howe Institute is an independent, non-partisan, non-profit research and education institution. It carries out, and makes public, independent analyses and critiques of economic policy issues, and translates scholarly research into choices for action by governments and the private sector.

The Institute was established in 1973 by the merger of the C. D. Howe Memorial Foundation and the Private Planning Association of Canada (PPAC). The Foundation had been created in 1961 to memorialise the late Right Honourable C. D. Howe, who served Canada in many elected capacities between 1935 and 1957, including as Minister of Trade and Commerce. The PPAC was a unique forum created in 1958 by leaders of business and labor for the purpose of carrying out research and educational activities on economic policy issues.

While its focus is national and international, the Institute recognises that Canada is composed of regions, each of which may have a particular perspective on policy issues and different concepts of what should be national priorities.

A Board of Directors is responsible for the Institute's general direction and for safeguarding its independence. The President is the chief executive and is responsible for formulating and carrying out policy, directing research, and selecting staff. In order to promote the flexibility and relevance of its work, the Institute's high quality professional staff is intentionally kept small and is supplemented with a number of scholars and compatible institutions.

Participation in the Institute's activities is encouraged from business, organised labor, trade associations, and the professions. Through objective examinations of different point of view, the Institute seeks to increase public understanding of policy issues and to contribute to the public decision-making process.

Jack M. MacLeod is Chairman and Maureen Farrow is President and Treasurer.

The Institute's offices are located at: P.O. Box 1621, Calgary, Alberta T2P 2L7; and 125 Adelaide Street East, Toronto, Ontario M5C 1L7 (Tel. in Toronto, Ontario M5C 1L7 (Tel. in Toronto, 416-865-1904).

Publications of the British-North American Committee

BN-36 *The GATT Negotiations 1986-1990: Origins, Issues and Prospects,* by Sidney Golt, November 1988 (£6.00, U.S.$10.00)

BN-35 *Stiffening the Sinews of the Nations: Economic Infrastructure in the United States, United Kingdom, and Canada,* by Simon Webley, December 1985 (£4.00, U.S.$6.00)

BN-34 *The Process of Innovation,* by Nuala Swords-Isherwood, October 1984 (£5.00, US$8.00, CAN$10.00)

BN-33 *Governments and Multinationals: Policies in the Developed Countries,* by A. E. Safarian, December 1983 (£4.00, $8.00)

BN-32 *Trade Issues in the Mid 1980s,* by Sidney Golt and a Committee Policy Statement, October 1982 (£3.50, $7.00)

BN-31 *The Newly Industrializing Countries: Adjusting to Success,* by Neil McMullen, November 1982 (£3.50, $7.00)

BN-30 *Conflicts of National Laws with International Business Activity: Issues of Extraterritoriality,* by A. H. Hermann, August 1982 (£3.00, $6.00)

BN-29 *Industrial Innovation in the United Kingdom, Canada and the United States,* by Kerry Schott, July 1981 (£2.25, $5.00)

BN-28 *Flexible Exchange Rates and International Business,* by John M. Blin, Stuart I. Greenbaum and Donald P. Jacobs, December 1981 (£3.00, $8.00)

BN-27 *A Trade Union View of US Manpower Policy,* by William W. Winpisinger, April 1980 (£1.75, $3.00)

BN-26 *A Positive Approach to the International Economic Order, Part II: Non-trade Issues,* by Alasdair MacBean and V. N. Balasubramanyam, May 1980 (£2.25, $5.00)

BN-25 *New Patterns of World Mineral Development,* by Raymond F. Mikesell, September 1979 (£2.25, $5.00)

BN-24 *Inflation is a Social Malady,* by Carl Beigie, March 1979 (£2.00, $4.00)

BN-23 *A Positive Approach to the International Economic Order, Part I: Trade & Structural Adjustment,* by Alasdair MacBean, October 1978 (£1.75, $3.00)

BN-22 *The GATT Negotiations 1973-79: The Closing Stage,* by Sidney Golt and a Committee Policy Statement, May 1978 (£1.50, $3.00)

BN-21 *Skilled Labour Supply Imbalances: The Canadian Experience,* by William Dodge, November 1977 (£1.50, $3.00)

BN-20 *The Soviet Impact on World Grain Trade,* by D. Gale Johnson, May 1977 (£1.75, $3.00)

BN-19 *Mineral Development in the Eighties: Prospects and Problems,* a Report Prepared by a Group of Committee Members with a Statistical Annex by Sperry Lea, November 1976 (£1.50, $3.00)

BN-18 *Skilled Labour Shortages in the United Kingdom: With Particular Reference to the Engineering Industry,* by Gerry Eastwood, October 1976 (£1.50, $3.00)

BN-17 *Higher Oil Prices: Worldwide Financial Implications,* a Policy Statement by the British-North American Committee and a Research Report by Sperry Lea, October 1975 (£1.50, $3.00)

BN-16 *Completing the GATT: Toward New International Rules to Govern Export Controls,* by Fred Bergsten, October 1974 (80p, $2.00)

BN-15 *Foreign Direct Investment in the United States: Opportunities and Impediments,* by Simon Webley, September 1974 (80p, $2.00)

BN-14 *The GATT Negotiations, 1973-75: A Guide to the Issues,* by Sidney Golt, April 1974 (£1.00, $2.00)

BN-13 *Problems of Economic Development in the Caribbean,* by David Powell, compiled from a study by Irene Hawkins, November 1973 (80p, $2.00)

BN-12 *The European Approach to Worker-Management Relationships,* by Innis Macbeath, October 1973 (£1.00, $2.50)

BN-11 *An International Grain Reserve Policy,* by Timothy Josling, July 1973 (40p, $1.00)

BN-10 *Man and His Environment,* by Harry G. Johnson, August 1973 (40p, $1.00)

BN-9 *Prospective Changes in the World Trade and Monetary System: A Comment,* A Statement by the BNAC, October 1972 (30p, $.75)

BN-8 *Multinational Corporations in Developed Countries: A Review of Recent Research and Policy Thinking,* by Sperry Lea and Simon Webley, March 1973 (80p, $2.00)

BN-7 *Sterling, European Monetary Unification, and the International Monetary System,* by Richard N. Cooper, March 1972 (40p, $1.00)

BN-6 *Multinational Corporations and British Labour: A Review of Attitudes and Responses,* by John Gennard, January 1972 (80p, $2.00)

BN-5 *The Strategic and Political Issues Facing America, Britain and Canada,* by Leonard Beaton, October 1971 (40p, $1.00)

BN-4 *Purposes and Prospects,* A Policy Statement describing the BNAC, April 1971 (20p, $.50)

BN-3 *British Entry to the European Community: Implications for British and North American Agriculture,* by John S. Marsh, together with *Agriculture Policies for World Trade Expansion,* A Statement by the BNAC, March 1971 (50p, $1.25)

BN-2 *Transatlantic Relations in the Prospect of an Enlarged European Community,* by Theodore Geiger, November 1970 (60p, $1.50)

BN-1 *An Overall View of International Economic Questions Facing Britain, the United States and Canada during the 1970s,* by Harry G. Johnson, June 1970 (40p, $1.00)

Occasional Paper-5 *New Departures in Industrial Relations: Developments in the U.S., the U.K. and Canada,* April 1988 (£4.00, U.S.$7.00)

Occasional Paper 4 *Tensions in U.S.-E.E.C. Relations: The Agriculture Issue,* by Sir Richard Butler and Thomas Saylor, December 1986 (£2.00, U.S.$3.00)

Occasional Paper-3 *Managing Product Innovation,* The views of five BNAC members: Carrol Bolen, Ken Durham, Walter Light, Chester Sadlow and Viscount Weir, October 1984 (£1.50 US$2.00, CAN$2.50)

Occasional Paper-2 *Managing the Response to Industrial Decline,* by Joseph L. Bower, September 1984 (£1.50, US$2.00, CAN$2.50)

Occasional Paper-1 *New Investment in Basic Industries,* prepared by a Committee Task Force, June 1979 (60p, $1.00)

Publications of the British-North American Committee are available from:

In Great Britain and Europe	In the United States of America	In Canada
BRITISH-NORTH AMERICAN RESEARCH ASSOCIATION	NATIONAL PLANNING ASSOCIATION	C. D. HOWE INSTITUTE
Grosvenor Gardens House,	1616 P Street NW,	125 Adelaide Street East,
35-37 Grosvenor Gardens,	Washington, DC 20036	Toronto, Ontario M5C 1L7
London SW1W 0BS	Tel: 202-265 7685	Tel: 416-865-1904
Tel: 01-828 6644	Fax: 202-797 5516	Fax: 416-865-1866
Fax: 01-828 5830		